The Second Room
on the Right

The Second Room on the Right

LINDA JOYCE

CHAPEL HILL
PRESS, INC.

ISBN 978-1-59715-099-6
Library of Congress Catalog Number 2013952173

Second Printing
Printed in the United States of America

DEDICATED TO MAMA

One sweet Georgia peach

This book is a memoir. It is a book of true stories based on my best recollection of events and times shared with my family growing up in Atlanta, Georgia. A full lifetime later, my remembrance of things is scant and scattered. The things I remember, I remembered in great detail. The things I remembered in detail are perhaps the ones that taught the greatest lesson.

The greatest lesson I have learned is that many may never grasp the value of the black experience.

CONTENTS

PROLOGUE

When we lose our memory of the past, we no longer know one another. How can we know one another if we have never learned one another's stories?

ATLANTA, GEORGIA, 1960

A lot of living took place in the house on Arcadia Circle. If only those walls could talk, they would tell different stories of each of my ten siblings. To this day, none of us have ever referred to it as a home, just a house. This six-room shotgun shanty had three rooms on the left and three on the right. The three rooms on the right were bedrooms. The second room on the right belonged to me, Lettie, Henry, Gary, and whoever else needed a place to sleep at any given time. Your bedroom was the only place that you had a right to be, even if that right was shared with three other people at the same time.

The houses in the neighborhood were close. The one next door was so close that I could hear the dishes being placed on the wooden table at mealtimes. I am sure they could also hear everything that went on in our house, especially the nights when the beatings occurred.

On one such night, I stood in my bedroom naked, clothed only in the certainty of the inevitable. Daddy sat on the side of the bed, with his legs spread wide and his right hand gripping the razor strap. Fear made the air thick. His sweaty body made the air hot and musty. The pee-stenched mattress made breathing difficult. My two younger brothers and an older sister huddled in a corner, guarding themselves from the blows directed at me.

Daddy demanded that they be there, to learn the lesson that I refused to learn. All my siblings had been victims of his barbaric punishment for misbehaving. But after only one savage beating, each had vowed never again.

I, however, had been his victim many times. I was headstrong and stubborn. Tonight I was a victim once again.

My cry for mercy started long before my clothes fell to the floor, long before I closed the door behind me. I pressed my skinny frame against the back of the door in a conscious effort to put distance between us. This was also a subconscious effort to transport myself, as if by magic, to the other side of its hinges. Both efforts were futile. As my knees began to buckle, I begged him to please let me keep my panties on. But he always said, "No, I don't buy clothes to tear them up!"

He knew he would tear them because he knew he would tear my skin. That was his goal, and I felt it long before I saw the blood. I was forced to get on my hands and knees so that he could lock my head in his fleshy calves. This assured that I couldn't run. My body trembled when the fiery razor strap seared my skin. The more I squirmed, the tighter his headlock. The swiftness of his razor strap made the air whistle, and any blow that did not break my skin left welts that pulsated with pain long after the beating stopped. He stopped only when he saw blood, a lot of it. I could hear Mama in the background screaming, "Melvin, you're beating her too hard. If you don't stop, I'll call the police!" But her threats to call the police did not deter him. We all knew the police wouldn't come. We all knew that was the way it was—in the South, in the '60s. Back then, the white police didn't run to the aid of black children in distress. There was no way for any of us to know that one of the children in that room would be running afoul of the law for the next fifty years.

I was ten years old, weighed eighty pounds, and was strong willed. He was my father, 300 pounds, and a drunkard. I vowed to hate him forever. I didn't know that forever would only last for thirty-three years after his death.

The walls at 97 Arcadia Circle have begun to talk.

PREFACE

When daytime talk-show queen Oprah Winfrey launched her legendary book club in 1996, it didn't take long for the book club craze to spread worldwide. That was about two years after our book club came to be in Greensboro, North Carolina. Unlike most book clubs, ours was formed to improve race relations among women. For me, this book club did much more. In almost every book I saw bits and pieces of my life, played out in another time, in another place, with another face. Discussing the struggles of others gave me the freedom and anonymity to voice my own. Our book club agreed on one thing: Everyone has a story to tell. Reading far more books over the last fifteen years than I had read in my entire life has prompted me to tell my story.

What's more difficult, putting your past in perspective or putting it into print? For many years, several stories deep inside me have yearned to be given a voice. At times, the voices were so loud that my forehead felt like a flashing billboard. Other times a caution sign warned me to consider another path. Purging the soul is good, but when you pick at old scabs, they sting and threaten to bleed again. The picking burns and brings back old, wretched memories that I had prayed and hoped were long forgotten. Dipping my toe into the river of retrospection was easy. Putting the past into print proved to be more difficult. But the wounds are now open and the healing has already begun. I invite my readers to walk along beside me rather than view me from a distance.

I had already moved to North Carolina and had recently married when I began to get regular phone calls from Mama. At the age of seventy, Mama was strong, with a voice that was robust, reflective, and regretful when she said, "Just like I had no say-so in when I was born, I really thought that I had no say-so in how many would be born to me. I thought the Lord would make my body stop when it was time. I just had too many children for one person to take care of. I loved all my children, but if I knew then what I know now, half of y'all wouldn't be here."

That was the first time I heard her say she loved us. I'm sure she did but I never remember hearing it. I asked her how many would she have had if she could do it over again. She said, "Let's put it like this, Lin: You're number nine; you wouldn't have made it."

I half-smiled at the thought of not being born. But that was the kind of heart-to-heart chat that Mama and I would have many years after her child-bearing years were over, the kind of conversation that I wished we'd had when I was younger. In the late '70s, when a long-distance call was not free, Mama called me often. I rarely started the conversation. I seldom prompted the subject or asked any questions. What she talked about was not as important as the fact that she talked. There were so many things that I wanted to know, things I needed to know, jagged pieces that never fit, not enough water to drink, but more than enough to drown in. The camera in my mind produced many images, but none of them were in focus. Let me be honest, there were also things I wanted to tell her—one thing in particular that I needed to tell her again. She wasn't ready to receive it twenty years ago. Was she ready now?

One day, when she obviously had nothing much to say, she told me that she had put her life on hold for forty-three years. During those years, she rarely visited friends because she always had at least three or four children in tow at any given time. She never believed in shoving her kids on anyone else, so she simply stayed at home. If she took us with her, she knew that all adult conversation would be replaced with "Sit down, stop that, don't touch that, and put that down." We must have been the original Bébé's Kids. Mama said she longed for the day when we were grown and gone and the house could stay clean and quiet. She dreamed of the day when she could have some time to herself, time to do some things she wanted to do.

That day had finally arrived, and her dreams had turned to dread. Over the years she had become an expert at stretching a morsel of bread to feed many mouths. Now that she had more food than ever, she only had one mouth to feed. A clean house in the morning gave her nothing to do in the evening. If something was misplaced, there was no one to blame but herself. The quietness of her house was deafening. The spaces in her head were hollow. The combination of both was scary.

For more than four decades, she lived her life for and through her children. All the hustle and bustle, conflict, and confusion had once threatened her sanity. The absence of it all now left her vulnerable to the insanity ahead. Now that her children were gone, her house was too quiet. It was lonely. She needed someone to talk to.

Her thoughts, although deliberate, seemed snatched from thin air. They were random, but they were thoughts she wanted to share. On one occasion she said, "Lin, I remember the night you were born. It was on a Thursday and it rained."

As she talked, I recalled how she had worked until the last minute of each of her subsequent pregnancies. By now she had given me enough big pieces and the small ones stretched and filled the gaps, enough for me to relive the day I was born.

1950

A Rainy Night in Georgia

It was quarter to four in the afternoon and Mama had ironed the last creases from the white cotton pillowcase. Ironing pillowcases was what the white folks required, so she required her daughters to do the same. As a domestic worker for the last ten years, she knew what pleased the white folks. She knew she had to please them in order to keep her job. She had long since finished everything else that Mrs. Peterson had required and had done so in record time. By now her routine was more of a habit, a reflex. As she neatly refolded the morning's newspaper, she noticed the bold print in the headline:

"Fire Destroys Palmer Institute." Her brow furrowed as she read on: "Fire in Sedalia Wednesday destroyed the main girls' dormitory at Palmer Memorial Institute, a 49-year-old boarding school for Negroes. The girls lost all their belongings but no one was hurt. Dr. Brown said defective wiring caused the fire." The wrinkles on Mama's forehead seemed to smooth out a bit. A soft, warm breath of thanksgiving came from her lips, "No one was hurt. Praise God." In those days, black folks losing everything in a house fire was all too common. No one dying was uncommon. With eight children of her own at home she knew that the mischief of a toddler, the carelessness of teenagers, overcrowded space in a two-bedroom housing project, and defective electrical wiring that was all too common in almost every Negro dwelling meant that her family's name could be among the next victims in tomorrow's headlines.

In the bottom right corner of the newspaper, in smaller print, the weather forecast read, "Mostly cloudy and unseasonably warm, scattered showers in the evening."

The big print in the newspaper was an indication of what was important in everyone else's world. The big stomach beneath Mama's maternity top signified the reality of her world. For the last nine months, a tiny life force evolved as it kicked and grew inside her womb. Mama was growing full with her last daughter forming inside her as southern blacks were growing restless at dealing with the vestiges of Jim Crow. In eight days Huey Newton, a black boy from Monroe, Louisiana, would turn eight years old. In the decades that followed, Huey would become one of the founding members of the Black Panther movement that radicalized the civil rights campaign in America.

Today, four o'clock could not come fast enough. The clock seemed to stand still. Today, Mama's lower back ached as the weight of her distended belly pulled her forward. Her legs were still strong, but her feet were swollen. Mama prayed for her baby to wait just one more day. If she made it until Friday, her off day, she would have the two days to rest and be back to work on Sunday night without losing any pay.

FULTON COMMISSIONERS APPROVE PLAN
FOR NEGRO HOUSING UNIT
BY C. W. GREENLEA

Fulton County Commissioners Wednesday placed an okay on the rezoning of 40 acres of land . . . for apartment use. The property, formerly owned by Clark College and the Method-ist Church, will become the site of a 500- to 600-unit housing project for middle-income groups. . . . A group of white residents . . . opposed the use of the land for a Negro project.

When the clock struck four o'clock, Mama knew she had less than ten minutes to gather her things and make it two blocks to meet the No. 8 transit bus en route to the housing project where she lived. As she boarded the bus, three empty seats took on the life force of a giant magnet. The seats invited her tired body to take rest. That magnet was no match for the stronger kinetic pull of social conditioning and the Jim Crow law that led her straight to the back. It always seemed to be darker in the back of the bus. It seemed darker in the back, not because only blacks were crowded there, more because there was no laughter or chatter, like that coming from the front. As usual all the seats were taken, so she held on tight and thanked God for at least having a place to stand. At the next stop, the bus lunged to a sudden halt. Mama's grip was loosened, and she plunged forward into the lap of an elderly blind gentleman. Minding less about her delicate condition and more about intruding on someone else's space, she apologized as she regained her footing. The old man's instincts were sharper than his sight. He quickly stood and motioned for Mama to take his seat.

The pressure in Mama's lower back made the bus ride seem unusually long. When she thought about the grueling three-block walk from the bus stop to her three-room flat, the bus ride wasn't long enough. This was no time to think about small stuff because this weary sparrow had eight other younglings who anxiously awaited whatever she had to give at the end of the day.

Mama also worked as a maid, cleaning a large bank in Atlanta. She pulled the graveyard shift from eleven o'clock at night until seven o'clock in the morning. Five nights a week, after leaving the bank in the morning, she came home long enough to see that her children got something to eat for breakfast and got off to school. She then rushed to take the bus across town to clean the white folks' house until four o'clock in the afternoon. The evening treadmill in her house was a mirror image of the morning treadmill at the white folks' house. Two big differences: Mama's house was the final resting place of secondhand furniture and other hand-me-downs that had seen better days. All those items had seen better days at the white folks' house.

It was seven o'clock in the evening. After ensuring that her eight children had been fed and accounted for, Mama was always exhausted and sleep came quickly. Tonight, however, sleep didn't come easy. Mama had been down this road before, eight times before. The pressure in her lower back became a dull ache in her pelvis, and that rhythmic dull ache became more pronounced. Mama knew then that her unborn baby could not understand and cared even less about the lost wages that would result from an early delivery.

At ten o'clock that evening, when Mama would normally be preparing for another night of cleaning the offices at the Trust Company Bank of Georgia, she packed her brown paper shopping bag with a toothbrush, a jar of petroleum jelly, a pair of panties, and a head scarf and prepared herself for labor at the hospital. As Mama and Daddy began their two-and-a-half-mile walk to F. Earl McLendon Hospital, it began to rain, just as the newspaper had predicted.

At 11:03 p.m., in the second month, on the ninth day, Linda Joyce was born as the ninth child to Melvin and Mary Hill. Before her arrival, Melvin Jr. had been their firstborn. Two years later Ethel had arrived. She had been followed by Ralph, Janie, Sarah, Calvin, Charles, and Lettie, every two years, just like clockwork.

All of them were characters in a drama called life. The setting was Atlanta, Georgia, and the stage was 97 Arcadia Circle. Each brought his or her own script, along with the special effects.

WHERE I'M FROM
I am from
the earth, the breath and the image of God.
I am a
female child from the Black Race.
I am from the lineage of
Melvin and Rozzie Hill and Hamp and Etta Gray.
I am from the loins of
Melvin Albert Hill and Mary Gray Hill.

I am from
the hot dusty days of the South.
I am from
a housing project, a tarpaper shack and a shotgun house.
I am from
the rainy nights in Georgia.
I am from
the earth, the breath and the image of God.

Mama remembered the day I was born. I remembered the day Daddy died, at least the funeral. His funeral was typical of most in the black community. Everyone marched around the open casket to see him one last time. At the age of fifteen, I was tall, skinny, and so nearsighted as to be nearly blind. Squinting was now a natural reflex that compensated for my nearsightedness. As I approached the casket, I was careful not to get too close. I could feel the wrinkles form on my forehead as my eyes squinted just enough to bring him into focus. There he was in a black suit and tie with a white shirt, with that curious knot still standing out on his head. I stared so hard that I thought I saw him move. I jumped when someone from behind motioned me forward. This was the first time I ever saw him all cleaned up and dressed in brand-new clothes with nowhere to go. I didn't remember him ever being inside a church. This was also the first time that I saw his name in print, the first time I knew this much about him:

OBITUARY

Melvin Albert Hill was born in Macon County, Georgia, on September 21, 1910. He departed this life on July 15, 1965. He was one of eight children born to Melvin and Rozzie Hill. In 1932 he was united in holy matrimony to Mary Lee Gray. To this union eleven children were born. Melvin worked as a chef for The Southern Railway for thirty years. He leaves to cherish his memory, his wife Mary, and eleven children....

As the organist played "Amazing Grace" in the background, I was amazed at how it was not only an expected practice to stop short of the truth when talking about the deceased but it was almost mandatory to tell a lie. Who assumed that all his children would cherish his memory? I know I didn't cherish it. There was sadness all around me, but I wasn't sad. I was glad he was dead.

The twenty-two-year age span between the oldest and the youngest sibling explained why this was the first time all of us were ever under one roof at the same time. This would also be the last time. At the time, we were practicing Seventh-Day Adventists, and I knew the Ten Commandments well—especially the fourth one about keeping the Sabbath holy. I knew every precept and promise and could defend each boldly. The fifth one about "Honoring your mother and father" was simple enough, but I could never defend the part about honoring my father. All I could defend was hate.

Shame and justification jockeyed for their rightful place in my reasoning. Justification won. Surely there was an amendment or an exception to the Fifth Commandment somewhere in the Bible?

The church had no air conditioning; neither did the funeral car that transported us to the cemetery. The stifling heat of the July sun had no mercy on anyone in Atlanta and even less mercy on the twelve of us packed inside the black limousine. As the funeral motorcade snaked its way through the main drive of Lincoln Cemetery, a small crowd was already waiting near a mound of Georgia red clay. They were Daddy's coworkers. The only one I recognized was Mr. Avery. I wondered if they were more like Mr. Avery or more like Daddy. At the grave site, the mourners pressed their way toward the green canvas canopy covering the six-foot hole.

The smell of the sun-baked clay wafted in the air beneath the funeral tent. Mama cried softly, others cried openly. Tears filled many eyes. Hate filled my head. I hated him for the things he did to me and even more for the things he did not do for me. He was out of his misery and the misery of him was out of me, or so I thought. His casket was lowered into the ground, but all the disgust, anger, and hatred refused to be buried with him. I thought of the last time that he beat me. At that moment I vowed, "That was the last ass-whipping that I would ever take from any man." I struggled to find good memories to cherish. The ones I could not cherish, I struggled to bury. My struggles began early.

My oldest sibling, Melvin Jr., was sixteen when I was born. Mama rearranged our tiny apartment to accommodate nine children and two adults. I was only six months old when the Housing Authority learned that our family's size had increased. That was entirely too many people for our small quarters, they said, so we were ordered to vacate the housing project immediately.

Our entire family moved in with Grandpa Hill, who lived in a tarpaper house on Delbridge Street. This house was about four city blocks away from the home of Martin Luther King Jr. My brother Melvin Jr. was very smart. He skipped two grade levels and entered Morehouse College at the age of sixteen.

Our large family occupied two rooms on the back of Granddaddy's shack. On one side of the house, Granddaddy sold hot dogs, fish sandwiches, and fried chicken. On the other side, Daddy's sister had carved out her living space. Still another one of his sisters and her husband had a makeshift bedroom on an enclosed front porch. Granddaddy's house had a kitchen but no refrigerator. Folks waited for the iceman to come once a week, just as kids wait for the Good Humor man today. I can remember being very excited to be the first one to hear the clanging bell and see the old beat-up ice truck coming down the street. With a big, proud grin on my face I screamed, "Mama, the iceman is coming, the iceman is coming!" I recall an upright wooden container with legs and a metal latch called an icebox. This crude-looking contraption awaited a big block of ice that kept our meager food supply from spoiling in the heat of the southern summers. I never saw the iceman in the winter. I guess our house was cold enough to serve the same purpose.

In the 1950s, stress was an expected reality of black folks; so was having children. Finding warmth and comfort in your partner's bed was a natural and convenient way to relieve stress. Whenever you saw two adults, you saw at least two children. Sometimes the number of children that a couple had was an indication of how they handled stress. Our family was under a lot of stress and still growing. Soon our growing family required a move from my grandfather's house to the house at 97 Arcadia Circle.

❦ POISON ❦

Buying bootleg liquor was a common practice in the Deep South, where paying the expensive price and tax on legitimate whiskey was a burden for poor people. To save on the cost of distilling whiskey, a bootlegger mixed three hundred gallons of whiskey with a barrel of methyl alcohol. When his salesmen sold this toxic mixture throughout the black neighborhood, hundreds fell ill, seven were blinded, and thirty-nine died inside of a week. A superstitious black hospital attendant said that the mass poisoning was God's way of punishing bad colored people.

Daddy was not one of those "bad colored people." He was never known to be violent or even argumentative. His limited schooling made him no match for anyone who could reason or carry a thought to its next conclusion. Daddy made up and passed along jokes about ignorant Negroes and uppity Negroes who had no common sense. He delighted in his ability to make people laugh, mindless of the fact that he was the brunt of most of the funniest ones.

Unable to fight or voice a cry of dissent against the moonshine poisoning atrocity, Daddy used the same tragedy that brought tears of anguish to create jokes that brought tears of laughter. Telling jokes was Daddy's way of escaping his harsh reality of being a black man in the South. That was a common practice among blacks then and unfortunately still holds true today.

All the forces in the universe were aligned so that Daddy could have been one of the victims of the moonshine poisoning, but he wasn't. His greater torture was not being able to support his family, which drove him to drink—poisoning himself slowly but just as surely.

I put a thumbtack in Stanley Brown's seat. Served him right for talkin' 'bout the holes in my shoes. I punched skinny James Wilson in the stomach . . . only because he was the only one I knew I could beat. I yanked Jill Curry's long thick hair. I envied it but hated her for having it. So how did she get so lucky? Something about being part Indian. I fought a teacher and stole milk money. None of these ever seemed to be serious enough to warrant a trip to the principal's office.

Arcadia Circle, Where It All Began

❦ 97 ARCADIA CIRCLE ❦

Many of the stories that I've wanted to share were life-changing experiences that were born or nurtured in my birthplace of Atlanta, in a house on Arcadia Circle. The stories are about things that disturbed me, especially those things that seemed to faze no one else.

These stories happened long before I knew about instant coffee and integration, long before the world knew about the Internet, long before city streets were renamed for political activists and civic leaders, even longer before the Georgia Dome, the Underground, and the Spaghetti Junction became landmarks. Hunter Hills was the heartbeat of the collective black community in one of the most vibrant times in Atlanta's history. Burbank Drive was the main street that channeled people between Hunter Street and Simpson Road. Burbank Drive was the main artery that pumped lifeblood into the neighborhood surrounding Arcadia Circle.

Arcadia Circle was the longest of three streets that formed a circle that snaked around our neighborhood. The terrain of steep hills and sharp curves was symbolic of the struggling families that bordered its path, families climbing upward hills that they hoped would lead to a better place, never knowing where that place would be or whether they were on the right path.

I don't remember how I got there, but there I was, in front of this big house. Someone held my hand as we climbed the six concrete steps that led to the long wooden porch of our new house at 97 Arcadia Circle. A new house to most colored people in the South in 1954 was usually not new but more likely another old house in a new location. Although I was too young to have any complaints about the house we moved away from, this house just seemed to be much better.

The earliest known use of the term "shotgun house" was in a classified advertisement in the *Atlanta Journal*, August 30, 1903:

> Two 3-room houses near the railroad yards at Simpson Rd. crossing, rent $12 a month to good tenants who pay in advance; price $1,200 on terms or $100 cash, balance $15 a month; a combination of investment and savings bank.
>
> Wikipedia citation, contributed by *Moore v.*
> *Minnis*, 11 Tenn. App. 88 (Tenn. App. 1929)

These were not shacks but good shotgun houses in good repair. While this advertisement seemed to present shotgun houses as a desirable working-class housing alternative, by 1929 a Tennessee court noted that shotgun houses could not be rented to any other than a very poor class of tenants.

Our shotgun house was a shack with no indoor toilets or central heating. We did have a kitchen and obviously a refrigerator because I never saw or heard from the iceman again. Straight ahead inside the house was a long hallway that seemed to go on forever, one room following another and another. Ours was the only shotgun house on the street. The term "shotgun house" is often said to come from the saying that one could fire a shotgun through the front door and the pellets would fly cleanly through the house and out the back door. Our new dwelling, although dilapidated, was actually a "double-barrel" shotgun house with rooms on both side of a central hallway that allowed access to both sides of the house. My bedroom was the second room on the right.

❧ THE FLOOR ❧

The plank floor in my bedroom was always cold, even colder in the winter. There was never a rug to dress it up or to cover the large light spot in the middle, a spot worn thin by bare feet, feet that gathered splinters and left tracks. I never thought much about it. I took it for granted. The floor squeaked. It sagged but it did what it was supposed to do. The floor was the foundation for everything in that room. Like that floor, my own foundation in life was weak and squeaky.

I was a happy, scrawny kid with big brown eyes that squinted almost to a close when I smiled and a smile that showed two fewer teeth below my upper lip. Two dimples dug deep into my brown cheeks, cheeks that rounded out a smooth face. My hair was thin and short, some parts long enough to tie a ribbon on, but not long enough to make the ribbons stay.

Linda Joyce, age five

My pigeon-toed gait made you wonder if I had left my high-top shoes too soon. Just two years out of those high-tops, I skipped everywhere I went. The skipping stopped when I arrived at the corners of Ashby and Beckwith Streets, the house where Miss Dorothy lived. Everyone knew that the sight of that house made me cry. No one knew why.

My first memory of this house was the spring when I was four years old, the first time I was left in the care and control of anyone outside my family.

Miss Dorothy was a mean, heavyset woman with fair skin and reddish-brown hair. Cigarettes, saltine crackers, and a glass bottle of Coca-Cola were her constant companions. Although I never encountered anyone else in that house, I distinctly remember several photos displayed in frames on the coffee table and mantle. Early each morning Mama took me to her house. As soon as Mama was out of sight, Miss Dorothy locked me outside on the front porch. The front porch was sterile, clean-swept, and lonely. Tears and temper tantrums did me no good, but when they went on too long, I was taken to the backyard. The world was my playground, but this patch of earth was my prison. I was locked outside in a fenced backyard with no toys, no ball, no swing set, no jump rope, not even a stick to draw a hopscotch game in the sand. I was only allowed inside to eat lunch or to relieve my swollen bladder.

On one occasion when I came inside to use the bathroom, my tiny eyes moved quickly to capture images that I could remember when I returned to my backyard prison. I noticed a shiny frame that held the picture of a little girl. The girl appeared to be the same age as I. She had a wide smile like mine, and her eyes squinted closed like mine. She had long pigtails with two bows on each end. Her skin was fair like Miss Dorothy's. I assumed that one had to have long hair to have ribbons and light skin to have long hair. Perhaps this was the moment when I also assumed that since I had neither of these features, I was not good enough to stay in her house. That had to be the reason I was being treated this way. I stared at the photos so long that I momentarily forgot about my overactive bladder. When Miss Dorothy caught me looking at the photo, she accused me of lying just to come inside. From that day forward, every bathroom request was suspect and consequently denied.

On many days warm liquid ran down my legs and soaked the top of my socks after my requests to come inside had been ignored too long. At the age of four all my potty training was completely undone. My soiled underpants were just another excuse for her to torture me, so I sat in wet clothing all day. Sometimes I was almost dry when my teenage brother came to pick me up, sometimes not. He didn't notice, or perhaps he didn't even care. Not much more than a child himself, his only responsibility was to escort me safely home, wet or dry. Wet underpants became a daily occurrence. That was also about the same time when I began hearing Mama's daily reprimand, "Linda Joyce, you are old enough to know better."

I didn't know it, but something had changed at home. Daddy had begun to drink heavily. On any given day Mama came home only to find at least one utility had been disconnected. Who was in the frame of mind to ask me how my day was? No one wanted to hear why a four-year-old didn't want to go back to a babysitter. Isn't that what most four-year-olds say? I knew I could always climb into Mama's lap and everything would be okay, but even that changed. Mama had recently given birth to Henry, her tenth child. I was no longer the baby! The infant son, who now pulled on Mama's apron strings, would one day pull even harder on her heartstrings.

It was Miss Dorothy the babysitter who crafted the mold for my self-image. Boundaries were clearly recorded—if not on paper, most certainly in my mind. For the next twenty years my mental boundaries were set by the American paradigms of beauty—light skin and long hair. At a time when my environmental boundaries were expanding, I should have been cultivating a wide understanding of the world around me. Instead, I was preoccupied with the perceived limitations of my black skin. I was the youngest girl in my family, and for the next seven years I became defiant and stubborn. For many years after that, I reaped the benefits and consequences of both.

My brother Melvin was only one semester away from finishing Morehouse College. But he could no longer take the cramped, depraved living conditions at home and Daddy's strong arm of discipline, so he dropped out of school and joined the navy. My brother Ralph felt the same way, and he joined the navy at age sixteen.

One picture is worth a thousand words. The picture I have in mind was sepia, two by three inches, with creases and scratches. But the girl in the photograph had skin that was smooth as silk and black as coal. It was my oldest sister, Ethel. She never lived in the Arcadia Circle house and had few memories of it. I had even fewer memories of her. She was Mama's second-born and an unofficial surrogate matriarch whenever Mama was not around. By the age of eighteen she had changed many dirty diapers and had exchanged even dirtier looks with light-skinned blacks and pale-skinned whites. She had had enough of it all, enough to know she didn't want to see another minute of living in the South. I had no idea of the other indignities the South had already visited on her. On the day she graduated from high school, she boarded a train to New York, never to live in Atlanta again. I often wondered how she got the courage to leave all that she had ever known for a place she had never seen.

My brother Ralph lived on Arcadia Circle for only a short time, but he does have memories. Fanning flies was a common ritual, not only in our house, but in most southern homes with no window screens to keep them out. Ralph's deep sleep was disrupted one time as he fanned flies away from his ear. When he waved his hand across his face, the fly felt furry. Its weight was that of a pigeon-sized bird. His sleep was now on the edge of dreams and reality, and he could hear birds chirping outside the window. The chirping brought calm, a nibble brought pain. Ralph swatted at his ear to remove the irritant. It wasn't a fly; it was a rat!

As Janie, Sarah, Calvin, and Charles witnessed Daddy shrink beneath the weight of his responsibility, they suckled strength and determination from Mama, who took up his slack. Upon reaching adulthood, each of them moved away from 97 Arcadia Circle and returned only for occasional visits.

As of yet, none of my siblings had made their mark on the world, but they were all placing their feet on roads that would take them to a world far different from the one of their birth.

———

The newspaper beneath my freshly polished black and white saddle oxford shoes was still wet. Mama had already picked the lint balls from my pullover top and ironed the creases from my corduroy jumper. I could hardly sit still while she pulled the hot straightening comb through the last section of hair, hair that still had to be plaited and secured with a bobby pin. This was my first day of school, an official end to any more days at Miss Dorothy's house.

The first day of school was the Tuesday after Labor Day. Although I was still just four years old, my fifth birthday would come five months later in February, long before the next school year started. To describe me as a precocious child was an understatement. For the past year, I had become my sister's shadow, quickly absorbing all her schoolwork. Mama was also ready for me to start school for another reason. Her youngest child was now two years old, and there was not enough money to pay a babysitter for both of us. We didn't own a car and we seldom had the money to ride the bus, so on my first day of school, Mama and I already knew what our mode of transportation would be. For the short time that I had been on earth, I felt like I'd done as much walking as breathing. I was so happy that I skipped the entire trip nonstop. Mama was a fast walker because she had so much to do, but today she seemed to be walking more slowly than usual.

I was ready to start my new adventure, but ready for what? What would I do on the first day of school? What would it feel like? What would it look like?

As the big red brick building came into view, my tiny frame began to quiver. The school appeared to be a million times bigger than our house, certainly larger than anything I had ever seen before. The building sat about six feet below the grade of the street, and it consumed the entire block. As we walked down the steps toward the front entrance, the building's roof line disappeared from view. When Mama opened the large metal door, we heard the most horrific and blood-curdling screams come from inside. It actually sounded as if children were being beaten and tortured. The scene inside resembled Ground Zero. Neatly starched dresses and trousers were now crumpled and soiled, as children lay prostrate in defiance, screaming, "I wanna go home." Parents stood bewildered but determined and spoke in rehearsed tones, "It's going to be okay. I'll be back soon." Ribbons that once adorned pigtails were strewn wildly about the floor, some barely hanging on for dear life. This was what the first day of school looked like.

In the early '50s, there were no preschools, Head Start programs, or early learning centers. You were just plucked from the familiarity of family and friends and drop-kicked into the midst of total strangers and other little creatures who were just as scared as you. The first day of school was traumatic.

My feet, which earlier had briskly skipped toward a new and exciting frontier, were now ready to take flight back to familiar surroundings. My big brown eyes quickly filled with tears, and before I knew why, I became one of the screaming war casualties. After what seemed like hours of standing in lines and completing tons of forms, Mama learned from the school officials that since my fifth birthday would not occur by October, I would have to wait and begin school next year. Before I began, I was put out of school.

The walk back to our house was even slower than before, and I didn't mind, since we were going away from that school. Perhaps Mama needed that extra time to ponder her next move, because she was already six months pregnant with Gary, her eleventh child. Jokingly, Dr. McLendon said that if she had an even dozen, the twelfth would be free. Mama didn't think that was funny.

<hr>

White people lived in the largest houses in the suburbs with their luxury-fitted kitchens and washing machines, refrigerators, and much more. Almost everything about our own house, however, would violate today's building codes. Our front yard, the center stage for daily drama, also abutted one of the low-lying areas on the street. No city planning, bad water runoffs, and heavy rains were the perfect catalysts for backed-up sewer drains. A storm that lasted for more than twenty minutes resulted in a flood that submerged our street and yard beneath two feet of water. We delighted in stripping to our white cotton panties and wading in the brown murky waters that we called our private swimming pool. During a heavy rain, pots, pans, bowls, and glasses were placed wherever the roof leaked. If the leak was over our beds, we pushed the beds as far away as possible.

I traveled back to that neighborhood more than thirty years after I left and I found that not much had changed. It is obvious now how black neighborhoods came into existence. Blacks were only allowed to build homes on land that was unsuitable for whites.

The first winter on Arcadia Circle was brutal in more ways than the weather. In our house, two fireplaces had been built into the adjoining walls of the first and second bedrooms on each side of the hallway. This was supposed to enable the front and middle rooms to share a common chimney with a fireplace opening in each room, but the fireplaces could not be used. The flashing around the chimney was gone, and most of the shingles were missing from the roof. The fireplaces were no more than fire hazards. In those days, black folks losing everything in a house fire was common. Losing life and limb were common, too. At that age I was not required to navigate nightly visits to the outhouse, but I do remember something about a slop jar and my siblings being angry when I clumsily knocked it over in the mornings. Baths were taken in a large metal tub. All baths had to be started and completed immediately after dinner, while the heat from the kitchen potbelly stove still warmed the room. It was an awful way for many blacks to live.

If our house violated every housing code, it also may have been condemned, because several years later there was a frantic rush to make major repairs. We finally got an indoor toilet on the back of the house. The outhouse went away, but a chicken coop took its place. Many of the repairs were external and were made while we still lived in the house. Not much changed about the interior. The kitchen was reconfigured to accommodate more space for a refrigerator and sink. Part of the back porch was enclosed to make the kitchen large enough to accommodate a table.

❧ THE WALLS ❧

I remember the walls in the second room, four walls that stretched from the ceiling to the floor, walls that adjoined a wooden floor, walls that stood still and always stood tall, walls that enclosed us—walls that exposed all.

Mama was a pioneer when it came to quilting and recycling. Many hours were spent reducing salvaged fabric to small squares of cloth—an old towel, a corduroy jacket, a wool coat, a cotton blouse, denim jeans—no piece of fabric was spared. Every scrap of material was rescued and reused. From those squares, and with the aid of rusty scissors, a big needle, and black #8 thread, she crafted heavy quilts that kept us warm in the winter. Everyone had a quilt. Everyone needed a quilt to survive a brutal Georgia winter night. The weight of those quilts prevented us from moving once we got into bed.

Each quilt, unique in itself, was symbolic. The cotton blouse, the wool coat, or denim jeans had a separate and distinct purpose in their former lives. The swatches in the finished quilt represented all the colorful and sordid details of our lives.

Mama, age eighteen

Old rags and newspapers were used to stop severe drafts. We hovered close to stay warm, but we drifted further apart, trying to stay alive.

❧ MAMA ❧

Mama stood about five feet, four inches tall. She had smooth skin and big legs. By today's standards, Mama would be a tad overweight for her height. In the early '50s, Mama was a "brick house" with the prettiest smile that God ever made.

That smile began at the corners of lips that stayed closed and ended just below her beautiful high cheekbones that she thought unattractive, so she chose to take photos from a side pose. She was not a flashy woman, but a well-groomed, well-built woman with pride.

1955

School Daze

In the fall of 1955, when Martin Luther King Jr. had just finished seminary, segregation was alive and well in the South. The education of the Negro child was still a low priority for the Georgia legislature. As the size of black families grew, the number of educational resources and facilities failed to keep pace. When I was finally old enough to be admitted into the public school system, there was not enough classroom space to accommodate the city's need. Kindergarten students had to be educated in shifts. One shift began at seven-thirty in the morning and ended at eleven-thirty in the morning. The second shift started at noon and ended at four o'clock in the afternoon. As you might have guessed, I was assigned to the second shift. For decades, I assumed that it was because I was poor. Years later I learned that if your parent did not come early to request the morning shift, then the afternoon shift was yours by default. I was the only child in my entire neighborhood on the afternoon shift, by default but not my fault. Each day I came home to empty streets that had recently clamored with the sounds of hopscotch and kickball. My playmates, who by now were exhausted from the thrill of play, had retreated to their homes. I remember sitting on the curb, using my finger to draw images of children in the sand. This was my first school-related disappointment. The next one taught me a lesson.

I learned how to steal from a girl named Jill.
Jill got away, but I had to pay.

As first-graders, we paid little attention to clothes and skin color, but we still found ways to advance our social position. A classmate by the name of Jill had the longest and thickest hair that I had ever seen. She wore three pigtails, and whenever asked how she got such pretty locks, her reply was, "My grandma was part Cherokee Indian." Surely there must be at least one Cherokee Indian out there who is part Negro. To this day, I've never heard anyone gladly volunteer that information.

Everything in our elementary school was big: big windows that lined the opposite wall, a big blackboard that covered the front wall, a big rear wall to hang coats and other matter, a corner bathroom to relieve our tiny bladders. School is where I got into trouble that was equally big. I spent most of the day learning how to connect the dots and how to color inside the lines. The highlight of the day for me was lunchtime. At a designated time, the older students lined up and went to the cafeteria. All of us newbies ate at our tables after someone brought our small cartons of milk on a plastic tray. A nickel was the cost of white milk. That milk was enough to wash down my jellied biscuit wrapped in waxed paper. When the tray got to me, I proudly handed over the nickel that Mama had given me earlier that morning.

Some time later, chocolate milk was added to the drink selection. Not only did this become an instant rave, it also became another way to distinguish between "the haves and the have-nots," because it cost a penny more. An extra penny was impossible for Mama to contribute. Each day when the milk cart arrived, hands instantly flailed the air signaling one's desire and ability to purchase chocolate milk. When it became obvious that I was the only one still drinking white milk, I became the object of my classmates' teasing. I didn't particularly care for chocolate, but if everyone else wanted it, so did I. I suffered in silence as the repeated taunts made the highlight of my day unbearable.

Each day at least one person lost his or her penny and had to go without, everyone except Jill. One morning shortly after we arrived at school, I saw Jill take someone's penny. Next, she reached up and slid it beneath the thick clump of hair at the base of her long ponytail. Abracadabra and it was out of sight! I will admit that I was extremely jealous of Jill's hair, but now I was also envious that she had found a way to get her chocolate milk without her mama paying for it. It wasn't long before someone else was careless with their penny and I picked it up. Just like Jill, I quickly slid it beneath the plaited section of hair on the top of my head. I knew that it was not likely to move if I were careful. What I didn't know was, since my hair was so thin, the penny was also very visible. When my classmate began to cry about the loss of her money, the teacher came over to console her. When the teacher came closer, she saw the penny sitting in plain sight on top of my head. I was accused of the previous thefts and paddled severely. At the age of six, I probably knew that what I did was wrong but I could never understand why I got punished and Jill did not. I assumed it was because she had long hair. Jill got away and I had to pay.

The crotch of his pants was wet. I didn't know that there were few public restrooms for coloreds.

Daddy seldom came home, so early memories of him are sketchy. I vividly remember an incident at a community health clinic. I had been taken there to get booster shots. Waiting in the hallway outside this big open room, all I could hear from inside the Sunset Community Health Clinic was screaming and crying. While all the other children were accompanied by their mothers, Daddy came with me. Just the thought of vaccinations was scary to young children, so the crying began before they entered. The screaming really started once inside. When my name was called, Daddy took me inside and left almost immediately. I went through that terrifying ordeal all alone. When I was taken outside to reunite with the responsible adult, there was Daddy, standing in a small puddle. I didn't know that Daddy was a drunkard. I didn't know that peeing on yourself in public is what drunks do. I thought, maybe just like me, Miss Dorothy wouldn't let him go to the bathroom either.

Daddy, age twenty-two

❧ DADDY ❧

Mama told me that as a young man Daddy was the life of every party. He was a snappy dresser and a good dancer. No doubt those were the window dressings he used to over-shadow his third-grade education. He was a good cook and a charmer. He was so charming that at the age of twenty Mama said yes to his proposal, and they married in 1932.

Daddy had much in common with his buddies. They all had limited education, limited skills, and meager earnings that barely kept a raggedy roof over their families' heads. Joining the armed forces might have solved many of Daddy's economic problems, but when he was younger he successfully faked a disability to dodge the draft. Stories have it that his bowlegs made it easy for him to turn his feet inward and walk on his ankles. This obvious disability was how he was able to avoid the military. That was the first time to my knowledge that he exaggerated a physical condition to shirk his obligations. The next time he attempted to use a physical ailment as an excuse to avoid work, it would be his last time.

❧ SIBLING RIVALRY ❧

The age spread between us made my older siblings seem more like cousins because some had already moved away by the time I was aware of them. There were so many of us that we had to talk fast and loud in order to get anyone's attention. I'm still trying to break those two habits today.

We were all automatic babysitters for the next younger sibling. Punishment was swift and severe if the younger one got hurt or into trouble while in our care. Sibling rivalry was a constant game played by the last four of us: Lettie, Henry, Gary, and me. Lettie could be described as a tomboy. I was headstrong and stubborn. Henry was called "Jughead" because of a head shape and size that outgrew his body. Gary, the youngest, was born with a sleepy eye. He was a thumb-sucker with a round head like Charlie Brown. He looked like an old man.

I looked up to Lettie, and we were close. The only thing that separated us were the twenty-six months between our births. Where you saw one, you saw the other. We were an unlikely pair because she was thick and mischievous and I was skinny and gullible. We stuck together. As we got older, if she told a lie, I rubber-stamped it. If I told a lie, she cosigned it. Lettie thought up the shenanigans; I carried them out. Back in the day, our names were spoken as one— "Lettie and Lin"—kind of like the modern-day Thelma and Louise, except our pranks were more stupid than illegal. When we were old enough to know better, we were punished together. We got into trouble, played hard, and had big fun!

Once Henry came, I expected to have the same control and rule over him. The pecking order had been set, or so I thought. Although he was two years my junior, we stood eye to eye and he was physically stronger. My every effort to control or dominate him was matched with his successful retaliation. I often yielded in tearful retreat.

Henry was left-handed and stuttered when he spoke. These were two so-called abnormalities that we all thought needed to be and could be corrected. To correct his use of his left hand, we were instructed to give him a hard slap on that hand whenever he was caught using it. We teased him when he stuttered. He soon developed quickness to counteract our persistent hand slapping. He also retreated to secrecy, perhaps for protection from the teasing.

Always full of mischief and antics, he became an expert at irritation. As a child he was the ultimate practical jokester. He was quicker and stronger, so he terrorized me often. Henry had a nervous energy that kept him in constant motion. His nickname of "Jughead" seemed to be most fitting because there was always something brewing in his head that was not so obvious. None of us were remotely aware that he was developing a mind-set that would one day keep him out of step with society and one step ahead of the law.

Frantically the caller continued, "No, I'm serious. You got to see this. There's this dude pulling a car on a stolen tow truck and leading about twenty police cars on a high-speed chase on Interstate 20. They've closed off all exits, shut the highway down for miles, and the traffic is backed up to downtown. It appears that this dude stole a car from the police impound using a stolen tow truck. This cat is flying! They can't catch him!"

1956

Struggles

❦ THE WINDOW ❦

The window in the second room was double hung with a single pane. The top half was cracked. The lower half was cloudy. Both halves were dirty. Its latch had long been broken. One hand could open it easily. A brick or an empty can kept it open in the summer. Old rags and plastic kept it tight in the winter. Just beyond those panes was a panoramic view of nothing. Like the window view, my entire world was out of focus. I saw things much differently than most. I saw things that others never saw. Some things I never saw.

Everyone thinks I was punished more than most. For obvious reasons, I agree. The best way for me to explain my wayward behavior is to recall what was going on *before* my behavior changed.

I truly cannot remember when and how I came to know that my eyesight was impaired. As a child I don't ever remember getting an eye exam. If I did, certainly nothing was ever done with the results. As an awkward, nearsighted adolescent, my distance vision was limited and blurred. I broke everything I touched. Every time I ate food I dropped crumbs on the floor. When given a command, I responded slowly. My slothful behavior seemed to signal that I was lazy, trifling, and at the very least rebellious. While I'm willing to admit

27

that some of that may have been true, a greater blame can be attributed to my extremely poor eyesight. Any visually impaired person will agree that a large part of audible communication is aided by sight. When I could see a person's body language, facial expressions, even eye movements, I could anticipate what was about to be said and respond almost instantaneously.

> January 30, 1956—Martin Luther King Jr.'s Home Was Bombed
> On Thursday, December 1, 1955, Rosa Parks refused to give up her seat for a white person on the bus she took on her regular ride home from the Montgomery Fair department store. After the successful beginning of the boycott, the Montgomery Improvement Association (MIA) came into being that afternoon, and Martin Luther King Jr. accepted the presidency. As MIA leader, King became the focus of white hatred. On January 30, 1956, the King home was bombed. (CNN LIBRARY)

Martin Luther King's name was heard every day on the radio and television but I heard something different. For years I called him "Martha Luther" instead of "Martin Luther."

I stumbled over objects and I could not discern the body language of anyone at a distance. If I couldn't see them, I couldn't understand them. The time lapse between these interchanges was probably nanoseconds. When this was happening twenty-four hours a day, every day of my life, much anxiety resulted. This became my reality, my normal. Back in the day, if your parents gave you a command, you were not supposed to analyze now and respond later. Your responsibility was to jump quickly. For obvious reasons, I never responded quickly enough. My impaired vision caused many more problems at school.

Poor vision was the most difficult obstacle to learning. Sharing a limited number of secondhand textbooks usually didn't present a problem for me because I was usually paired with someone who didn't want to learn anyway.

I remember a common task that was always fraught with frustration: copying information from the blackboard, which was impossible because I simply couldn't see it. This was especially problematic because my seat was in the back of the room. I never knew how classroom seating was assigned, but we were given orders, not options. While the teacher was writing, the only audible sounds were the shuffling of notebook papers and the hiss of white chalk screeching across the wall slate. Then without warning, the stillness would be pierced by the scrubbing sound of my desk being pushed across the tile floor. Suddenly all the attention was fixated on me as I awkwardly maneuvered between two rows and up the main aisle, tripping over book bags and anything else in my path. Once I was seated near the board, the class returned to normal. That, too, was short-lived because any information written on the board that was more than an arm's length away required that I get up and move again. The entire class would burst into laughter. The teacher would be openly disturbed, and I was ultimately humiliated. While the class was in an uproar, this was an opportunity for someone to poke fun at my shoes, my faded sweater, or my ashy black skinny legs.

One day I was taunted unmercifully by a boy named Stanley Brown. I decided it was time for him to feel the pain. He asked for permission to go to the back of the room to sharpen his pencil. As usual when he returned to his desk he would stand and wave his newly sharpened pencil in everyone's face. At the very last second before he took his seat, I placed a thumbtack, point up, in this chair. He plopped down into his chair with a macho attitude, but he jumped, holding his butt with a sissy scream. Once again the class burst into laughter, but I was paddled severely and sent to the principal's office. I got a whipping at school, then another whipping at home. Of course Mama's whipping hurt, but not as much as Stanley's teasing.

Poor vision wasn't the only malady that zapped my enthusiasm for learning. Many days I was so hungry that I was lightheaded. Everybody in our house was hungry, so I guess we couldn't blame the rat for nibbling on Ralph's ear.

Amid all the daily chaos, Mama constantly tried to instill in us social graces and good manners. She said, "Always say, 'Yes ma'am' and 'Yes sir,' 'Please' and 'Thank you.'" She was forever scolding us for belching out loud and passing gas in public. In retrospect and perhaps in resignation, Mama probably would have just settled for us acting civilized. I used to think we were much like scavengers, looking to put anything in our mouths to ease the knot of hunger in our bellies. I thought Mama was crazy to think we would really follow her instructions to share our food and ask our playmates to "Have some" if it was mealtime. Half of a lifetime later, a childhood friend named Elaine Jenkins recalled that Mama shared anything we had. She especially remembered eating Mama's good biscuits.

❧ MY STRUGGLE WITH STUPIDITY ❧

Mama never thought we were stupid, but she knew we did stupid things. Perhaps she figured that if she taught us with a saying, it would be easier to remember and more likely to be adhered to. So she raised us on sayings. Some may think her sayings were a bit vulgar for a Christian woman, but when all was said and done, she knew that the Lord would only hold her responsible for raising her children. If she thought a choice word here or there would make a difference, she didn't hesitate to use it.

One of her colorful sayings was, "A needle and thread can close any hole, and soap and water can clean shit." Although we were poor, Mama instilled in us that being poor does not mean you have to be dirty and ragged, and she repeated this saying often. There was never any excuse for dirty and ragged clothing. When we were younger and money was scarce, we only had the one change of underwear. We were instructed to take our panties off before going to bed, wash them with soap and water, and hang them to dry. She made sure she had washed enough for the two younger boys. Every morning when Mama came home from her night job, she lined us girls up for panty inspection. If our panties were torn or dirty, we got two whacks on our head from her shoe heel.

On any given morning, the sound of the push on the front door was an indication that Mama was home from her night job. It was a push of urgency because she only had a short window of time in which to make certain that we were all dressed, fed, and off to school before she left for her daytime job. I required more time because at the age of eight I was still a bed wetter, and "No child of Mama's was going nowhere smelling like pee." One morning, I had already finished my morning bath before I realized that I had forgotten to wash my panties the night before. Fearful of the certain wrath of Mama and the pain of her shoe, I quickly washed them at the last minute. I wrung the panties in a towel and hoped she wouldn't notice they were still damp. Mama could smell the urine-soaked mattress from the hallway. When she entered my room, the air was instantly thinned by the crosswind that swirled from the opened window. For some reason Mama inspected me first. When she lifted my dress and observed that my wet underpants were sticking to my narrow bottom she whacked my head twice with her shoe. I left home with wet eyes and underpants, but both were usually dry by the time I arrived at school.

On still another occasion when I failed to wash my panties, I decided to steal my younger brother's underwear and pass them off as my own. It was only after I felt the four whacks from Mama's shoe that I realized that the front opening on the underwear gave me away. Several weeks later when I failed to wash my panties again, I tried the boy's underwear trick once again. This time I turned the front opening around to the back, hoping she wouldn't notice. Mama was furious! This time the punishment was eight whacks to my head, just for being so stupid to think she was stupid. She hit me so hard that one of my plaits became undone. For some unknown reason she became more incensed when she thought I tried to outsmart her. That morning I left for school with a dry bottom, but my hair was standing on top of my head.

Years later my brother Gary shared that he remembered crying because one day Mama made him go to school wearing girls' underwear. That probably was one of those days when I was pulling so many shenanigans with the underwear that Mama decided to just let it be. I can still hear Mama saying, "What if you are in an accident and the people at the hospital saw holes in dirty underwear?" Never mind the possibility of death or being seriously crippled, her constant creed was still the same: "No dirty underwear!"

As far as I knew, Mama meted out punishment to the younger kids. I found out later that as the boys got bigger, their discipline was left for Daddy. At a young age I was required to fetch my own switch. Mama said, "Get three so I can plait them together." She knew one would break. She whipped me often. She thought I deserved it.

The school year went by fast. The summer went by even faster. With no community centers or parks nearby, the newly paved streets were the playground of all baseball, kickball, and hopscotch games. We were often and openly disturbed when a car or truck interrupted our play. Our lives were in constant danger when cars rounded a blind curve or found us playing just beyond a crest. We occupied and amused ourselves with everything.

My three-year-old brother Gary wandered upon a large corrugated box. He found this contraption interesting because it was light enough to push around, it was large enough for him to hide in, and most of all no one else seemed eager to take it from him. One day a large truck was descending the hill approaching our house. The driver saw a cardboard box sitting in the middle of the street. The driver's first inclination was to straddle it and leave the remains for someone else to discard. At the last minute he decided to stop his truck and move the box to the side of the street. When he lifted the box, to his surprise, inside he found my brother Gary fast asleep.

Daddy began working with the Southern Railroad Company in the late 1930s. Many freedmen willingly abandoned sharecropping for the lucrative railroad jobs, and the southern railroads relied on Negroes because they knew that workers who were used to performing slave labor were less likely to complain, regardless of the rigors of their work or length of their day. It was a good job. The railroad and the post office were two great jobs for unskilled colored men. The post office was attractive because of the level of stability and the government benefits. However, all applicants were required to take and pass a civil service exam, and Daddy couldn't read. The railroad didn't require a written test, so this job was a better fit for Daddy.

In the early 1930s Americans were still scared and leery of the talk of airplanes, so rail service thrived as the best way to travel. When Daddy began working with Southern Railway, life was grand. The work was steady. The long hours made the pay good. His gift for gab made the tips easier to get. The average tip started as a nickel, although pennies were handed out, too, usually two at a time. When the standard tip became a dime, Daddy came home with a loaf of bread for everybody! On his way home he would stop by the butcher and buy five pounds of chicken feet and a bag of rice. When tips were better he brought large cans of sorghum syrup, crates of eggs, flour, and sugar.

Years before I was born, finances were good, and Mama was able to send her children to a private school, but that was when she only had four children. Later, fewer were choosing rail travel and more people were flying. Daddy's tips were down and our family size had more than doubled. Daddy felt trapped.

❦ "OWE MY SOUL TO THE COMPANY STORE" ❦

When Mama realized there was no way of ensuring that Daddy's paycheck would make it home, she opted to use the company store. The Southern Railroad operated an employee store called Sands. This store sold everything from food to clothing to appliances. Sands was similar to our present-day Costco. Instead of it being a discount store, it was a high-end store. The prices were openly and undeniably five times higher than other merchants. Someone later told me that this was the brainchild of one of the stockholders, perhaps a way to keep money flowing in one direction, back into their hands. Employees and their families could shop on credit, and the money would be withheld from the employees' pay before they received it. This was Mama's last resort because she'd spend an entire week's paycheck only to get one-fifth the money's worth of food. When Daddy got a pay stub with little money left to buy booze, he was arguably upset, but what could he do about it? When he found other ways to get a drink, he missed days at work. When that happened, Mama's spending privileges were suspended because the account was overdrawn. The hunger cycle would begin again.

Open cracks and crevices in our house were the gateway for rats and roaches. Comedians tell jokes about folks with roaches. Believe me, those are no jokes. For several years we had roaches, but when they could find no food, they moved on. The rats were more difficult to deal with. I have yet to hear a joke to describe what it's like to live with rats. The first rat I ever saw was about seven inches long with a tail almost the same length. It was decades later before I knew that rats came in smaller sizes. We called them "waltz-rats." Unlike most rodents, they didn't wait to come out at night. They must have felt right at home. Our instructions for rats were to chase them into a corner and beat them with a shoe. Most of the time this worked.

On one occasion my sister and I chased a huge rat into a corner. With our shoes aimed high, my sister and I knew that this rodent was history. The rat knew it, too. Suddenly, the rat's survival instincts kicked in. With snarling teeth ready to bite, the rat reared up on his long tail and plunged toward us. Our own survival instincts kicked in, and we ran for our lives. To this very day, I've never seen a rat that big. I always thought that waltz-rats were a special species. I also thought they were named "waltz-rats" because they were big enough to dance with. Today I know that the correct name is wharf rats. They are one of the largest muroids—a brown or gray rodent with a body up to ten inches long, and a similar tail length. The male weighs on average twelve ounces. No one blamed the rats for nibbling on my brother's ear. The rat was just as hungry as we were.

❧ KIDS AT PLAY ❧

Unlike today, when I was a child there were no fancy games or high-tech toys to play with. Nonetheless, our hands and feet stayed in perpetual motion doing anything our little minds could conceive. Mama was forever warning us not to play with or to stay away from certain bad kids in the neighborhood. Little did Mama know that we taught the bad kids everything they knew!

Playing baseball was a common summer pastime. Our family size made this game a perfect fit because we already had enough for our own team. On one occasion, my brother Calvin was on third base, the bases were loaded, and a home run would assure a victory for our family team. When the plank bat sent the ragged tennis ball flying across the field, everyone screamed, "Run home, Calvin, run home!" In the excitement of it all, Calvin obeyed the crowd's command, and like a speeding bullet, he took off and ran toward our house. The louder we screamed, "Run home, Calvin, run home," the faster he ran home. His lanky legs became limber and his heels dug in the dirt. All you could see was a cloud of dust moving swiftly in the outfield. On that day, Calvin could have won an Olympic gold medal for the fifty-yard dash. Since the other basemen could not touch home plate until Calvin did, that gave the opposing team enough time to retrieve the ball. We lost the game. Calvin lost the second time when my brothers and sisters beat him up.

As were most backyards in our neighborhood, ours was deep and the ground sloped toward the house. Weeds and thick brush covered the rear section of the yard, and we called it the jungle. A persimmon tree separated the midsection of the yard, which was cleared for the clothesline. The foreground just beyond the back porch was where we played. That grassless patch of earth resembled the bald spot on an old man's head where hair refuses to grow. On the far right edge of that patch a mulberry bush stood. Whenever we thought we stood tall enough to look down on Mama, the plaited limbs from this bush produced the switches that she used to cut us back to the ground. A persimmon tree and mulberry bush were the only plants that blossomed at 97 Arcadia Circle. The bitterness of both is what I remembered most.

Our house sat on cinder blocks that were three feet high. The open crawlspace provided a cool playhouse in the summer. Since I was short enough to stand in most places and crouch in others, this was a perfect refuge from punishment because adults could not maneuver in such close quarters. I often had horrible nightmares of being chased by King Kong. For some reason, the lack of headroom in the crawlspace was no problem for him.

We probably invented recycling because any throwaway items that we found in our immediate environment resurfaced with a new purpose. A worn-out tennis ball was an ideal substitute for a baseball because it was lightweight and it eliminated the need for a catcher's mitt. Any two-by-four piece of wood with no nails in it served as a great baseball bat because its width assured that we had a good chance of hitting the ball. The bases would be any four objects big enough to see and weighty enough to be stationary against the wind. Small pebbles and buttons served as jackstones. A piece of Argo starch substituted as chalk to draw hopscotch lines in the street. We found several uses for broken clothes hangers, thread spools, toilet paper rolls, egg crates, empty cans, and burned-out electrical fuses.

Mama had her hands full and her watchful eyes alert to prevent us from maiming ourselves. There was no health insurance. We never thought about death, but I do remember a white man coming by each month to collect on a five-cent life insurance policy. I never thought about whom it covered. I wonder if the insurance coverage was really that cheap or whether the insurance company figured our lives were not worth more than a nickel. The insurance salesman came inside, careful not to touch anything or sit down. His wide eyes slowly studied us in amazement, as if we were creatures from another planet. Oddly, we were staring at him the same way.

Gary, Mama's youngest, spent many hours watching television and memorizing every commercial jingle. Henry was into all kinds of nonsense, Lettie was mastering street sense, and I was struggling with something Mama called common sense.

Once each year, we went downtown to buy shoes for school and church. Before we left home, we had to force every ounce of liquid from our bladders so that we wouldn't have to go again until we got back. Last-minute instructions were repeated, "Don't ask for anything and don't touch nothing!" My excitement was mixed with bewilderment as to why all the water fountains and restrooms had signs that said, "Whites Only." It seemed as if just reading the signs made me have to go. It angered Mama when we had to trek several long blocks back to a designated store and go down several flights of stairs, back in the corner, and behind a stockroom, all because of my anxious bladder. On future trips she left me at home whenever possible.

The Skin I'm In

During those formative years, I discovered that the concept of who I was, and what I could eventually become, was carved in my mind by forces or elements that were completely out of my control. No other members of my family ever expressed dissatisfaction with their skin color. After my experience with Miss Dorothy, awareness of my skin color did not resurface again until I started third grade. I thought I was considered not good enough to be in my peers' company because I did not have light skin. I had a plan to work on this problem from the inside and out. The internal plan was that I prayed secretly every night for God to wake me up the next day just a little bit lighter than when I went to sleep. The external plan was to scrub myself with Ajax scouring cleanser each night until I saw results. After only one night, I saw results. It worked! Or so I thought. In the morning when Mama came home from her night job, she said I looked just like an "ash cat" and rubbed me down with Royal Crown petroleum jelly from head to toe and sent me on to school. Somehow, the shine from that petroleum jelly made my dark skin look even darker. Now the kids had one more thing to ridicule me about.

How could I fix eyes that didn't see and control the color of my skin, the length of my hair, the clothes I wore, the house I lived in, or having a drunk for a father? I didn't ask for any of this. I hated my childhood. I hated the house we lived in. I felt trapped! No doubt Mama felt trapped also. Her life was also spinning out of control. Surely this was not the way she planned it. She rarely spoke of her childhood, but when she did, she spoke with teary eyes and a heavy heart.

Mama was born in 1912. Most women shy away from revealing their age, but Mama proudly announced that she was born the same year the *Titanic* sank! She was proud to have a connection with anything of importance, no matter how tragic, much like those today who boast of being born or married on September 11. Mama was twelve when her parents divorced. She said, "I begged Papa not to go. He was so good to me." Mama and her father actually bore a striking resemblance. Both had chiseled cheekbones. His eyes were flat, like fish eyes—like there was no light behind them, like Mama's eyes had recently become. The younger of two girls, Mama felt slighted. She thought perhaps she was an "oops baby," a bitter vestige of a sour marriage.

When her mother remarried, twelve more children were born to that union. Mama's stepfather and mother were so busy running numbers, drinking, and selling liquor that Mama was required to become surrogate parent to her new siblings. That was when Mama vowed to never put her children off on anyone else. All of her duties of washing, cooking, cleaning, bathing, and dressing her siblings had to be completed before she went to school each day. As a child, Mama loved school. School allowed her an escape from her reality, an escape to play "what if" and "if only" games in her mind. She often said, "I loved school and was good at it. I loved learning. I idolized the teachers who had so much knowledge because they received so much respect and admiration. I thought teachers were next to God. Teachers could do no wrong. At an early age, I knew that I wanted to become a teacher."

The Great Depression, which began as the decade of the 1920s ended, quickly made worse the economic and social conditions that had been bad enough all along. As unemployment rose, blacks, the last to be hired, were the first to be fired. Millions of whites suffered serious reverses for the first time in their lives. Millions of blacks simply sank deeper into despair. At the age of sixteen, Mama was forced to drop out of high school and was sent to work full time in the fields. With tear-filled eyes she recalled, "That was the hardest thing I ever had to do in my life. I begged Mama not to make me drop out of school. I cried and screamed and pleaded for her to let me get my diploma." But the death of a dream failed to bury the dreamer.

At the age of forty-five, Mama had just as many children as her mother. She spent her days cleaning someone else's home while her own house was in disarray. She was married to a man who drank and threw his money away by running numbers. She was keeping her marriage vows "until death do us part," but she hated the life she lived on this side of death. She went to church, she read her Bible, and she paid her tithes and offerings. Perhaps Mama agonized, *What did I do wrong? How can I do any more? What can I afford to do less of?*

Most of the families in the area had two to four children. Ours was the largest in the entire neighborhood. The Parish family of ten, which lived several blocks away, was the next largest. I think the Scotts at the other end of Arcadia Circle may have had just as many.

The two-year age spread between our eleven-child household likened us to an octopus's tentacles that reached to many quadrants of the city. Somebody always knew at least one of us. If they ever came to our house, they knew all of us.

The working women were domestics, and the men were unskilled laborers. If there was a caste system, their children didn't know it or didn't care because everyone came to our house to play. They always enjoyed coming because there was always something going on. If they were too timid to participate in our tomfoolery, they could just watch without being harmed or punished. Perhaps their parents also enjoyed sending them because it was much easier to call them home than to get rid of all of us.

I walked to E.C. Clement Elementary School each day with my sister Lettie. Our route was a combination of one dead-end street, several paved and unpaved roads, a railroad track, one steep hill, and two smaller embankments. Shortcuts were made by climbing fences and cutting across lawns. We opted to take longer routes if stray dogs roamed the area. Lettie viewed me as a tagalong, not a companion, so I had to keep up. A small neighborhood store, Warrior's Grocer, sat on the corners of Ackridge and Eason Streets—the only store between our house and school. The store offered a lot of things to buy but not much with our small amount of money. I never had more than a nickel.

Our lunch money was a nickel a day. That nickel bought ten two-for-a-penny cookies. By ten o'clock in the morning, hunger had driven me to sneak and eat eight of them. Eating those last two cookies at lunchtime was hard because I was surrounded by other kids who had plenty of good stuff to eat.

One day at lunchtime in Mrs. Eason's class, the ten cookies that I bought that morning were down to two. I knew it wouldn't take forty-five minutes to eat them so I sat, stared, and starved. Several girls had already arranged their desks in a private circle to share their lunch. Of course I was excluded because I had nothing to share. Although I was not close enough to see what they had, I was close enough to smell it. It was the one lunch item that kids boasted about: the ham sandwich. I can think of no other food that evoked our taste buds like the smell of cured ham. Ham had a way of making salt taste sweet. It gave salt a certain texture. It made salt seem less wrong and more right. It was the one food smell, like no other, that caused uncontrollable cravings. A ham sandwich for lunch was a sign of status. Inevitably someone would notice that I was all alone with no lunch at all. Instead of being invited to join them, I became the object of their teasing and jeering.

We were fortunate if we had any money to buy any amount of food. Whatever that amount would be would have to be enough. The frustrating part was that Daddy had a great income. The only problem was that it did not come into our house. The only way that we could get free lunch would be for Mama to leave Daddy so that we could qualify for a government free lunch. Well, that was not about to happen. First of all, she made a promise to God: "For better or worse and until death do us part." Squandering his income was probably the "worse" part, and she didn't know how long "death" would take.

No doubt many thought she was a fool to have that many children. She thought that taking handouts from the white man was just another form of slavery. To anyone who would listen, she'd say, "You may burn me for a fool but you won't get the ashes, too." This was another one of her sayings. This one meant, "I may have acted foolishly to have so many children, but I won't add insult to injury by asking you to help me care for them." She had no problem admitting, "I laid up and had all these children, and they are nobody else's responsibility but mine!" As a young child I hated her for allowing us to go hungry, just for the sake of keeping Daddy around. Mama wanted us to have more food, but she said, "Missing one meal won't kill you." She was right. We learned how to fast at a young age.

We seldom had enough food to stave off the hunger, but we had more than enough to keep us from starving. No matter how meager the meals were during the week, Mama scrounged enough flour and shortening to bake four dozen biscuits on Sunday morning. Buttered biscuits and Alaga syrup made us happy. The real treat came on the mornings she could afford to fry fish or salmon patties.

1958

A Bully Is Born

By now I knew how to handle sibling rivalry. I knew who was going to get me and whom I could get in return or at the very least how to avoid being gotten. What I wasn't prepared for were bullies. Unfortunately most people in the 1950s imagined bullies as outwardly troubled kids from low-income families or seedy circumstances. That was not true, and it certainly was not so for me.

Once each week all the students in my elementary school gathered in the auditorium for an assembly. This ritual was not for any particular purpose. Sometimes there was a special speaker or presentation. If not, we would just sit there for an hour. Perhaps this was the teachers' time to take a break, because whenever the laughter and chatter inside became too deafening, a teacher would appear from nowhere, quiet us down, and disappear again. The seating assignment inside the auditorium was simple. The lower classmen were seated up front and the next higher grades followed in succession. Back in the classroom my teacher instructed us to line up in an orderly manner in the hallway. All of us scrambled to be first in line. I was fast and could quickly secure a position among the first ten people, but then it happened. The light-skinned girls with long hair (who were not as quick as I) made promises of friendship if they were allowed to get in front of the line. Before I knew it, I was so close to the end of the line, I might as well have been the period at the end of a sentence.

The school auditorium was a large, open room. The wooden floor and high ceiling also allowed this to be used as a gymnasium. Large windows framed the side walls, and straight ahead stood a stage with red brocade curtains. A single aisle down the middle divided rows of gray and brown folding metal chairs. Our class was on the right side of the room. As luck would have it, since I was at the end of the line, I was on the last row for my class and grade. The last row of the third-grade class was right in front of the first row of the fourth-grade class, the row where Teresa sat. Teresa gave me my first taste of bullying.

The profile of a bully has not changed over the last fifty years. A bully is a coward, and because of that, bullies seldom act alone. Whether bullies act alone or in a group, a place of seclusion usually gives privacy to their acts. They are wimps in the face of authority. A bully targets only those of a smaller or weaker stature to lessen the chance of reprisal. A bully invites and enjoys an audience of peers so that the background cheers can fill the hollow cavities in his head.

The season was ripe and the scene was set for Teresa. Once inside the auditorium, the teachers disappeared. The crowd of at least 100 students provided the audience. Teresa was light-skinned, wore very stylish clothes, and was older and taller than I. I was her victim. I don't think Teresa was the school bully because I don't know if she targeted anyone else other than me. But "me" was all I cared about.

The anxiety of going to assemblies was the same I felt going to Miss Dorothy's. I was a little older, but I still felt trapped. As my classmates filed into the auditorium and filled the designated rows, I looked all around trying to spot Teresa before she saw me. Once seated I immediately looked around to see who was directly behind me. A sense of calm came only when I was certain that the person was anyone other than Teresa. Within minutes that calmness was replaced with calamity when I felt my metal chair being pulled back and my skinny body being folded up in its creases. Teresa had changed seats with the person directly behind me so that she could continue her torture.

Once seated, Teresa positioned her feet on the back bottom rung of my chair and pulled my chair backward. My lightweight frame easily slid back, causing the chair to fold with me inside. The crowd burst into laughter at the sight of a pair of legs, a pair of arms, and a nappy head being sandwiched in the folds of a metal chair. Only when the laughter reached a fever pitch did a teacher return, at which time Teresa released me from my torture chamber. As soon as the teacher left, Teresa repeated the torture again, inciting the laughter once again. I pleaded for her to stop, but my pleas were ignored. I threatened to tell the teacher, but she knew it was my word against hers. The one good thing about assemblies was that they were held at the end of the day.

Only two years before I couldn't wait to go to school. Now I couldn't wait to leave that place.

Teachers and students looked forward to the weekly assemblies; I no longer did. On one occasion I opted to just stand along the wall for the entire hour. Eventually a teacher appeared and instructed everyone to stay seated. On still another occasion I called Teresa's bluff and told the teacher. She was right. No one believed me. This hell went on forever. I was caught totally unprepared on the day it stopped.

There are several things that a young child cannot know about the evil practice of bullying. Two things I did not know: What was my boiling point, and what would I do when I reached it?

The assembly on this particular day proved to be frustrating, because it turned into a game of musical chairs. I had already talked with several classmates and asked if they minded switching seats once the teachers left. Several agreed to do so. Teresa was one step ahead of me because she had friends who agreed to switch with her also. Just as she was about to refold me into a chair for the fifth time, I jumped over the back of that seat and lit into her face. My arms were swinging like the broken limbs on a toy soldier. I was hammering her face hard and fast because I didn't know when she would answer my blows with hers, but she never did. I had caught her completely off guard. The element of surprise had stunned her. That was my ace in the hole. The crowd was now going wild with frenzy. The embarrassment of it all took away some of her steam. When the teacher arrived I was still slugging away, just in case. I was immediately ushered to the principal's office. Long story short, the verdict was rendered without even the suggestion of a trial. The sentence was swift. I was paddled by the principal, and then my teacher ordered me to write 200 times, "I will not fight in school." Mama believed all teachers were next to God. Since they were always right, I also got a whipping when I got home. Mama got even angrier that I would have to waste her hard-earned money by using notebook paper in this manner. Wouldn't you know it? The teacher had a desk full of blank notebook paper that was reserved just for troublemakers like me. There was never any for students who needed it to aid them in learning their lesson but always more than enough for students who needed to be taught a lesson.

That night back in my room, the second room on the right, my fingers cramped as I scribbled, "I will not fight in school." Several other things happened. My penmanship improved, I learned how unfair life is, and I learned that I could not depend on anybody else to protect me. I had to protect myself.

My skin was not as light as theirs, my hair was not as good as theirs, my clothes were not pretty like others', my classmates taunted me, and no one seemed to care. At night I lay in my bed, and I no longer liked school. It wasn't at all like I thought it would be.

At the beginning of each school year, the obviously unprepared teachers engaged us in the show-and-tell activity of "What I did on my summer vacation." No one wanted to hear that I played kick the can and stayed in the swimming pool until my black skin turned blue. Neither did I want to hear about when a classmate's whole family drove to see Grandmother in Miami, Florida, made castles in the sand, collected seashells, and made a scrapbook. First of all, my whole family had never done anything together, and we had no car to drive. Not only did I not know anyone in Florida, I had never been out of the state of Georgia. The largest sand piles I had ever seen were the mounds of sand that we emptied from our shoes each night, and the small pebbles in that sand might have been seashells. On the few occasions when I had something exciting to share, the teacher allowed the girls up front, the light-skinned and long-haired ones, to talk endlessly, and no one else had a chance to speak.

I had never known Daddy to give us any birthday or Christmas presents, so

I was overjoyed when I learned of his plans to take us on our first vacation to New York. Next time I'd have something to share. What happened during that trip on the following summer is a story that I would never tell because it would be a story straight out of hell.

❧ RIDING THE RAILS ❧

Daddy's month-long railroad runs took him from Atlanta to Washington, DC, and New York. This was the only real traveling he would ever do. One of the employee benefits that A. Philip Randolph fought for was free travel privileges for the workers' families. Now that we could ride the train free, all we needed was some place to go and a place to sleep when we got there.

Over the years, Daddy had met and served many passengers in the dining car. It was there that he met a classy and well-traveled Negro gentleman from Brooklyn, New York, by the name of Lanier Thrasher. His nickname was Pete. Pete loved Daddy's cooking and his jokes. Daddy loved Pete's generous tips. Pete regularly visited his family in Atlanta, and a brotherly kinship between Daddy and him evolved. We soon referred to him as Uncle Pete. Uncle Pete extended Daddy an open invitation to visit with him in New York at any time. The timing was perfect. This trip would be a first for me: the first time I rode a train, my first vacation, the first time going out of the state of Georgia, and the first time going to New York. August was a hot month in the South and the asphalt jungle of New York was even hotter, but I didn't know that my trip to the Big Apple would be derailed in hell.

The Peterson family, my mother's employer, had planned a two-week vacation, and Mr. Peterson had suggested that they give Mama a two-week paid vacation also. It was the husband, Mr. Peterson, who suggested the perks and the special breaks. Preparation for our trip began weeks before, just in case. Mama believed in "just in cases." The night before, four heads had been washed, eight knees and elbows had been scrubbed, and our clothes had been mended, washed, and ironed. She didn't know whether she was allowed to pack our clothing in paper bags so she borrowed luggage, just in case. The surface of the hard-body suitcase was textured by scratches, dings, and nicks. Mama knew there were bound to be last-minute items, so she readied two paper shopping bags, just in case. The suitcase's interior top elastic pocket had long lost its elasticity, and the lower section was marred with a few water spots. The two metal latches worked, but they needed a little caressing to close. A leather belt would be strapped tightly beneath the plastic handle, just in case. Daddy assured us that meals would be free because there were usually leftovers from each meal in the dining car. In a brown paper bag Mama packed biscuits and salmon croquette patties, just in case.

We arrived early at the Union Station. The taxi driver never stirred while we unloaded the backseat, but he did lean over the front seat to reach for his fifty-cent fare. Inside the terminal we followed Mama down a flight of steps that led to an underground network of tracks, trains, platforms, and people who policed the comings and goings. We climbed aboard after a white man took our tickets and directed us through a heavy accordion-type door on the left. Inside the trolley-like cabin, a narrow aisle divided sixteen rows of seating. Each row had two seats with straight backs and rawhide covering. The lower bottom of each forward seat provided a footrest for passengers behind. Only a handful of passengers occupied the cabin, none of them white. Perhaps this cabin was designated as "colored only." Lettie and I sat in one row, Henry and Gary sat in another, Mama sat across the aisle to keep a watchful eye on us all, just in case.

At the crack of dawn, the Crescent No. 4800 was given clearance to leave the terminal. The silence in the crisp morning air was pierced by the train's deafening whistle and the conductor's cry of "All aboard!" The rolling cabin lunged forward. People on the platform waved good-bye as we inched forward and houses and trees slowly moved backward. Once again Mama repeated her instructions: "Don't touch nothing; sit still and be quiet." We were excited, and Mama was anxious. Lettie and I whispered to each other. Mama whispered a word of prayer, just in case.

❦ DAYBREAK ON THE OUTSKIRTS OF GEORGIA ❧

Air-conditioned comfort was now a standard feature of rail travel, and the hissing sound of cool air from the overhead vents was an indication that it was working. Windows that were sealed closed gave me a panoramic view of the countryside. As the scenery changed from row houses and parked cars to farmhouses and tractors, the rising eastern sun thinned out the early morning darkness. Lettie constantly slapped Henry's left hand, and cool musty air hissed through overhead vents. Henry snatched Gary's thumb from his mouth, and Mama constantly shushed, "Stop that!"

We had just pulled into Toccoa, Georgia, when the conductor appeared and announced the breakfast menu. I sat on the edge of my seat and leaned my head into the aisle, anxiously awaiting what I thought would be our turn to visit the diner.

It had been more than an hour since the breakfast call had been made. Now my empty stomach growled louder than the vented air above. Finally Daddy appeared in the doorway and waved us forward. Mama gathered our things and guided us to the diner. After staggering through two heavy doors, we saw the third one open up into a sea of tables draped with white linen tablecloths. Each table was flanked by four metal-based cushioned chairs. On each table a lone rose rested in a small crystal glass. We sat at one table where Mama held Gary in her lap and each of us took the remaining seats. As soon as we were situated, the train came to an abrupt stop. Daddy looked startled, and his eyes suddenly widened with suspicion. Within seconds he turned around and left the diner. We thought he had gone to get our food. About thirty minutes had passed and not only had Daddy not returned but the conductor and several other men rushed through the diner. Something had happened.

Daddy was the next to appear in the doorway, and he hurried us back to our seats. Daddy disappeared, never to return, until the end of our trip. Once again Mama seemed anxious. She whispered a word of prayer, just in case.

Just outside of my window, a dozen of the train's crew scurried back and forth. Several of them crawled underneath the train; others huddled in deep discussion. When they disappeared, the train lurched forward once again en route to our northern destination.

Thirty minutes later, it was obvious that the train had not gained any speed. It was also obvious that we would not eat from the diner or feast on the much-expected white folks' leftovers. Mama opened her brown bag and gave each of us a salmon biscuit.

The temperature outside was fast approaching the high nineties as the Crescent approached the Spartanburg–Greenville, South Carolina, terminal. All of us had fallen asleep, aided by the rising temperature inside our cabin. As of yet the stickiness of our clothes and the sweat on my brow was not a signal that the train was in trouble. I looked over at Mama. Her eyes were wide open. That's when I knew there was trouble. The hissing of the air vent had stopped. The train's air conditioning system had stopped working. Without ventilation due to the sealed windows, the air inside quickly became thin. All of the colored crew was summoned into action to individually fan each white passenger.

All four of us begged for a bathroom visit, but Mama was afraid to move, so we couldn't move either. Coasting along at a snail's pace, it took us forever to reach the High Point, North Carolina, station. We were gasping for air, my clothes had become sticky, and my hair had begun to nap.

When the train pulled into High Point, the white passengers from the other cars bled out onto the platform. The hot air that gushed from beneath the train pushed them farther from the tracks. It was obvious from their expressions that they were just as uncomfortable as we were. They appeared to be revived just by breathing the outside air. For some reason no one was allowed to use the bathrooms on board. So the passengers hurriedly rushed inside the lone brick building to relieve themselves and to drink cool bottles of soda. Instinctively I jumped to my feet anxious to do the same. Mama snatched me back to my seat, telling me to wait until Daddy told us it was okay. This was her first train ride, and she depended on Daddy. He knew what to do, and he needed to know where to find us. As of yet, Daddy had not come back. Suddenly the train jerked forward and the conductor cried, "All aboard." Mama's eyes could no longer hide her fear. Perhaps her bladder needed to be relieved as much as ours. As the locomotive picked up speed heading toward Virginia, I noticed Mama had closed her eyes and had begun to pray. Lettie, Henry, and Gary slept soundly as beads of sweat glistened on their foreheads. Once again my eyes welled up as fast as my bladder.

Mama was already on her feet when the train got to Danville, Virginia. We had not seen or heard from Daddy in more than two hours. She may have doubted that he was even aboard. Nevertheless, she had decided that we were definitely getting off at the next stop. By now everyone else was wide awake and ready for a bathroom break also.

As soon as the train slowed and we were given permission to get off, Mama rushed us inside the transit building seeking a bathroom. Once inside the terminal, the large white sign with black letters, "Whites Only," answered her question long before she asked it.

Mama had seen many of those back in Atlanta, and she knew exactly what to do and where to go. Turning on her heels, she led us back outside to a wooded area about 200 yards across the dirt road. As we relieved our swollen bladders, Mama kept watch for our protection, just in case.

We rushed back across the road so as not to miss our train. This time the train stayed in the station several hours longer. Help had arrived. The malfunctioning air conditioning system had been repaired. The remainder of the trip was long and uneventful, but not as long as before. The week ahead would be even longer. Daddy reappeared by the time we arrived in New York.

Black folks who left the South thought the living was better in the North. I'll bet none of them were black children. Everyone knows children need dirt. There was no dirt in New York, at least not on the ground. There was no ground in New York, only concrete. There I sat on a concrete stoop. Back home we called this a step. Beneath this stoop, other people lived. The only things that lived beneath our steps were bugs and worms. I never knew how many families lived beneath the stoop or above it. I think it was many more than the number of people who lived in our house on Arcadia Circle.

Uncle Pete's family lived on the third floor, and that's where I spent my first two days in New York. Every building on that street was an apartment.

Every apartment was old. This old apartment building was located on Bedford Avenue. I don't remember the address, but I do remember that it was close enough to hear the crowds cheer from a huge baseball stadium. Those were happy sounds, but the sounds of New York were not always happy, especially at night. The third floor made the apartment safe enough to open the windows at night, but the stale air that rushed in brought with it the cries of the city, cries that sounded like people walking and running, talking and laughing, people dealing and stealing. The sounds of sirens screaming and fading in the night were enough to let Mama know that she needed to keep us close in her sight at all times. When Uncle Pete convinced her that it was safe for us to play on the stoop, she gave her permission, with reservation.

Going outside to play in Brooklyn was not as simple as it was in Atlanta. In Atlanta we had a long hallway that gave us an easy and quick access to both the front and back yard. Here in Brooklyn there was no long hallway, only long flights of steps that gave access to more steps but still no front yard or backyard. In Atlanta we had doors that never locked. In Brooklyn, not only did the doors automatically lock you out, but you could not come back in unless someone inside buzzed you back in.

Thirty minutes of idle sitting on the gritty concrete stoop seemed to trigger my anxious bladder. No one ever buzzed me back in quickly enough, so I hated going outside. This was the first time that I longed to be back on Arcadia Circle.

❧ SPECIAL TIMES ❧

We rarely got many toys for Christmas but that never stopped me from hoping and praying that each year would be different. Although I knew from an early age that there was no Santa Claus, I still went to sleep hoping for a miracle on Christmas morning. I'd get up early and find no trace of Santa or toys, and the remainder of my holiday was a nightmare. At the very least, Mama baked several pound cakes and several coconut and pineapple cakes.

One year our finances must have been better than most, because I woke on Christmas morning and the living room was strewn with all kinds of toys, gifts, dolls, trains, you name it. I was so surprised and happy that I just cried and peed on myself.

The day after New Year's Mama looked down and saw me struggling to get the jack-in-the-box toy opened. In frustration, I banged on the top several times before the Jack popped up. She turned my head to align her eyes with mine and said, "Don't you grow up to be no jack-in-the-box—you hear?" It would be more than a decade later that I learned what that saying meant. That kind of Christmas never happened again. I will forever cherish its memory.

The kids in our neighborhood knew how to celebrate Christmas, and celebrate they did. The neighborhood streets twisted and curved, dipped and dove like a huge roller coaster. On Christmas morning, it seemed as if God pulled the switch on a giant fun machine and it all came to life. In those days few toys required batteries or an electrical charge. Almost every kid got a pair of skates.

The beginner skaters got a pair of Union Hardware roller skates. The Unions were lightweight metal that had leather or plastic straps that secured them to your shoes. The wheels made a clacking noise when you pushed your feet forward to make them roll. Although the Unions tired you out quickly, they assured that you stayed on your feet longer while trying to get the hang of skating. The more experienced skaters got a pair of Fly-Away roller skates. Fly-Aways were made of a heavier metal. Instead of straps, each pair came with a skate key that resembled a ratchet. This key was used to tighten a metal clamp around your shoe. Once secured, the only way to become separated from your skates was to tear the soles from your shoes or tear your foot from your leg. The wheels had ball bearings that gave your skates a faster and quieter glide. God must have known that our shoes already had holes in the bottom and our parents had no insurance because I don't remember any broken bones.

❧ SKATE TRAINS ❧

An indication as to when you were good enough to hang with the big kids was when you graduated to Fly-Aways and could be a part of the skate train. The skate train was made up of ten to twelve skaters who lined up and held onto each others' waists. The most experienced skater was the engine; the least experienced was the caboose. No one wanted to be next to the caboose, because if the caboose fell and did not let go, the entire train could derail. Because the streets were steep, the skate train could reach speeds of twenty to twenty-five miles an hour. The only sound you could hear was the roar of the human train as the engine instructed you to "Rock, skate, roll." The crowds screamed in amazement. Without helmets or kneepads, this train was as dangerous for its passengers as it was to the spectators. I can recall several injuries and one death that occurred when a runaway skate train plowed into a parked car or a crowd of onlookers.

❧ VISITS FROM AUNT NELL ❧

Mama and her sister Nell were extremely close. Aunt Nell lived in Chicago, but she made regular Greyhound bus visits down South each year. She also made the best German chocolate cake in the world, which was her treat to us. She couldn't count on us having working utilities and cake ingredients on hand, so she baked the cake before she left Chicago. I can still see Aunt Nell waiting at the bus depot with her stockings knotted below her knees, a church hat on her head, a pocketbook on one arm, and a cake wrapped in waxed paper under the other arm.

Aunt Nell's given name was Easter Nell Johnson. She believed you should always try to live up to your name. Since hats are worn on Easter, a church hat was a standard part of her everyday dress ensemble. Like my oldest sister, she left the South at an early age, and she enjoyed telling about all the advantages of living in the North. Decades later I learned that Aunt Nell's housing situation was far worse than ours.

Aunt Nell's visits were a big deal. At least one annual visit was certain, but if a family member died or if Mama needed her, she came more often. She thought nothing of enduring a twenty-four-hour round-trip bus ride just to enjoy forty-eight hours with Mama. She came on weekends, on Mama's off day. Much like teenagers they spent many hours reminiscing and catching up. Late at night, their chatter often faded to Aunt Nell's mindless monologue and Mama's soft snoring.

At the age of eight I still played close to home. The Wyatt family, several houses away, had three girls. The Culpeppers, who were two houses in the other direction, had two boys. The neighbors without children had no patience for our taking shortcuts across their lawn. I never could understand why Big Joe Carmichael scolded me for cutting across his backyard since I always tried to walk on the piece of dirt he never used. Miss Bridges and Miss McCoy, the two spinster women across the street, constantly complained when our ball landed in their yards. It seemed that runaway balls were much like secondhand cigarette smoke. Both seem to gravitate to the people who least enjoy them.

Young Teachers/Old Mamas

Long before assessment testing came into vogue, I strongly suspected that students were grouped and assigned to certain teachers primarily on the basis of their economic standing in the community. The way you dressed and your parent's involvement in the PTA were the primary indicators of that standing. This practice allowed teachers to push students who had the potential for making it and to placate those who didn't. By now, you know which side I was on. Forty years later, a friend who was on the other side confirmed that my earlier suspicion was right on the money.

Monthly PTA meetings were the big to-do in those days. These were parent-teacher meetings, and students could come along only if the teacher allowed it. Today, they are called PTSA meetings, and the student is not only invited but also involved. I never knew whatever else went on at our PTA meetings. It must have been important because I knew that my classmates received special attention after the teacher saw that the parent was concerned enough to show up.

The meetings were held on a Tuesday night. I wanted so much for Mama to attend so that I could get the teacher's special treatment. Mama didn't come. She couldn't come, because she worked day and night. I remember one spring when Mama must have been on her one-week vacation. Once again, I begged her to attend a PTA meeting. When Mama said yes, I attended my first and only PTA meeting. Like a puppy, I scampered back and forth trying to get my teacher to notice Mama and me. The teacher never did. In this Parent Teacher Association it seemed that the teachers decided the parents whose association they wanted. I was crushed, but Mama seemed okay. Perhaps she only came to please me, not them anyway.

The torture was just beginning. As we headed home, I was sure that this one encounter would not give me the special privileges or standing that I thought were the benefits of belonging to the PTA.

The next morning at school, I was determined to salvage the evening before. I rushed to a crowd of my classmates, certain that this would get me the brownie points I had lost less than twelve hours before. I announced that my mama had come to the PTA meeting the night before. Suddenly one classmate shouted, "Yeah, and I saw her. She was old. You got an old mama." Everyone broke out in laughter and began to taunt and tease me. I was dazed. I never knew my mama was old. Wasn't she the age she was supposed to be? What was the right age for your mama if you were nine years old? Up to this point, I never knew or cared about my mama's age. She was my mama. She got here first. What did I do wrong? How could I fix that? From that day on, I never asked or wanted Mama to come to another PTA. I didn't need her adding to my pain.

———————

Another classmate named Carolyn (not her real name), who lived in another neighborhood, was the object of the same kind of teasing I endured. One day after school, I went to her house to play. Carolyn came from a large family, and her mama looked just like mine. It was then that I realized that raising a lot of children made you look old. When her mother came to the school the same group of girls began to taunt her, shouting, "You got an old mama." Carolyn burst into tears, ran home, and refused to return. The next day Carolyn's mama returned with her distraught daughter in tow. Upon realizing why Carolyn got so upset, the teacher became completely undone—not because of the rude, ill-mannered, and bratty teasers, but because Carolyn got so upset over something so petty.

I had to endure another type of bullying or teasing. Several teachers found it ridiculous and downright amusing that my mama had so many children. On any given day, when they huddled in gossip sessions outside of the teacher's lounge, one of them would ask, "Tell me again how many children your mother has?" As soon as I answered, "Eleven," they would all burst into laughter. Once again I thought, *Is that my fault? How can I control or correct that?* This happened so often that whenever the question was asked, I hesitated and said, "I don't remember" and quickly walked away, counting my fingers. I made sure that I was out of sight long before I got to the tenth digit.

❧ BOUNDARIES ❧

Opportunities to expand my boundaries came quickly. Doors closed even more quickly. I missed all class field trips because we couldn't afford them, even the ones that were free. Chartered bus services were hired to transport us to different functions, and the cost was two dollars. Two dollars was my total lunch money for two months. I had a choice—field trip this month but no lunch money for two months. The choice was painfully easy. As my classmates climbed onto the waiting bus, expecting the excitement ahead, I was sent to another teacher's class and instructed to put my head on my desk until my class returned. I can never recall any other child who stayed behind except me. Perhaps they were sent to another teacher. A tour of the Coca-Cola bottling plant, Grant Park Zoo, the science museum, a local bakery, or the symphony assured each participant a souvenir. The pain started anew when those goodies were dangled in my face when my classmates returned.

❧ MY STRUGGLE OF STUBBORNNESS ❧

Mama had the same cleanliness requirement about our house as she did about our bodies. Cleaning the house seemed hopeless because it never looked perfectly neat and orderly. With so many people living in such close quarters, something was always out of place. The girls were responsible for the inside of the house, and the boys were responsible for the yard. This arrangement was problematic for us girls and always provoked fights because the boys could wreak more havoc on a clean floor than we could on a dirty ground.

If I provoked Mama, the punishment was swift. On one occasion the swiftness and the provocation collided. I was about to begin a terrible practice that most would find unthinkable. This practice is unfathomable and unimaginable to every parent and one that would bring me within inches of my life.

Instructions from Mama had been clear. They had been itemized. They had been repeated several times, each with the promise of severe consequences for noncompliance. Mama said, "Clean the bathroom as soon as you get home from school. Make sure there is no ring around the tub. Pick up wet towels. Clean the toilet and sink. I'm telling you up front so you won't stick out behind" (another one of her sayings). Somehow, it was always my behind sticking out.

Hopscotch was my favorite pastime, and both feet had just landed on the seven and eight when I looked up the street and saw Mama coming home from work. Mama saw me also. Perhaps she thought, *Nine years old, still young enough to play hopscotch but old enough to handle household chores.* She believed her girls needed domestic training early in life. She got hers at an earlier age. The cadence of Mama's steps was swift and determined. Her body leaned forward as if to assure that her mind got to the house long before she did.

Shortly after entering the house, I heard Mama scream, "Linda Joyce, get in here!" My nickname was Lin. My brothers called me Lin-Pin because of my skinny legs. Mama was the only one who called me Linda Joyce, and that was only when I had done something wrong. Knowing I had done no wrong, I did not respond to the first command. The next command, much louder and more frantic, prompted me to go inside. As soon as I crossed the threshold, a fistful of knuckles slammed my head against the doorframe! Mama rarely meted out punishment with her hands. Those had to be preserved and protected to work and keep food on the table. Today Mama was livid and didn't take time to get a switch. Before I could regain my footing, Mama came closer and each blow was delivered with a verbal reminder of the unfinished task. "Didn't I tell you to clean that bathroom?" In reply I screamed, "But, Mama, I did clean it!" From this point forward, Mama's every retort was punctuated with a deliberate lick. She shouted, "*No—you—did—not. That—bathroom—is—still—dirty!*"

At that moment, my brain shifted into rewind to recall that I *did* clean the tub, toilet, and sink. Next it shifted to fast-forward trying to figure out why Mama thought it wasn't clean. Then it shifted quickly back to the present to dodge the painful blows. In the present is where my mind stayed, as I screamed and cried for mercy, inching backward down the hallway.

My back finally reached the opened door of my bedroom, the second room on the right. The frantic effort to barricade myself behind a closed door was unsuccessful. My frail body kept the door closed momentarily, then Mama's swift kick opened the door and sent me flying across the room. My head made contact with the metal bed frame, which explained the knot that later appeared over my right eye. To escape another lick I scampered beneath the bed. Just as Mama grabbed one of my legs to pull me out, my right leg jabbed back, striking her in the stomach.

Mama perceived this as retaliation. In shock Mama shouted, "You lil skinny youngun, you gon' disobey me, tell a bald-faced lie, and now you think you gon' hit me back?"

Now I had been falsely accused of three things I didn't do. To this day I don't know whether my next act was one of self-defense or a last-ditch effort to get her to stop and listen to me. Adrenaline rushed to my head and short-circuited my brain. Before I knew it or knew why, I slapped Mama in the face so hard that I twisted my wrist. Her eyes and mine widened simultaneously, hers in shock, mine in fear. The catfight that followed was ugly.

Mama's indignation was frightful. My flailing hands and feet soon gave way to the certain knowledge that I may not get out of this alive. After about five minutes of pure hell, Mama staggered with exhaustion and I lay lifeless in a crumpled heap. She picked me up and threw me in the bed and shouted, "Now stay there!"

For several minutes, Mama sat at the kitchen table fuming over what had recently happened. I lay in my bed whimpering. I couldn't sleep. I was confused. Everything happened so fast. Only minutes before, I was outside playing hopscotch. Now I was here in bed hurting.

I slid off the bed. Not bothering to find my shoes I inched my way down the hall into the kitchen, where Mama was preparing dinner. I walked quietly over and stood beside her for several minutes. After it appeared that her attention was elsewhere, still determined to get the last lick in, I brushed against her and touched my finger on her thigh. Today parents practice "time-out." Back then the practice was "knockout." Mama knew me well enough to know that the seemingly casual touching was my stubborn way of retaliation. In despair she looked down at me. With venom in her voice she said, "You think you're slick, but you can stand a little bit more greasing" (another of her sayings). "Girl, I will beat the devil out of you!"

Before those words could pierce the air, Mama stepped outside of herself and stepped inside of me. I don't remember much after that except that I may have been knocked unconscious because I fell into a deep sleep for about thirty minutes.

Most parents today would no doubt become totally unglued at the thought that a nine-year-old child—one they had given birth to, clothed, fed, and cared for—even harbored the thought of hitting back while being punished. I will be willing to wager a large sum of money that the only thing that prevents many parents today from exacting the same level of punishment would be the knowledge that not only would someone call the police but also that the police would come.

The evening sun from the open window was casting a ray of light across my forehead when I finally woke up. Slowly I walked into the kitchen where Mama was talking on the phone. No doubt she had been discussing my behavior. I walked over to Mama and rested my head on her thigh. The caller must have asked how I was faring. The whites of Mama's eyes were yellow and tired. She looked down at her strong-willed girl child, knowing this simple gesture of touching was yet another attempt to get the last lick. She responded to the caller, "I've never seen a child like this one."

In the midst of confrontation Mama found clarity. In resignation and perhaps in fear that she had been pushed to a dangerous edge of rage, she sighed, "She's sitting down on the outside, but she is still standing up on the inside!" (another one of her sayings).

Later that night we found out that one of the boys had dirtied the bathroom after I had cleaned it and left it in shambles. I don't know what she said to my brother, but she never apologized to me. Perhaps she thought I didn't deserve an apology because I fought her back.

Yeah, I got mad with Mama. There were many times when she beat me to within an inch of my life, but I couldn't stay mad long. Mama was my lifeline. Mama was all I had. Mama was constant and consistent in her discipline and demands but sometimes to a fault. Never mind that she had eleven children with eleven different personalities, eleven different brains, and hundreds of different needs. Never mind that girls had different needs than boys. She'd say, "Y'all got the same mama and daddy, I feed y'all the same food, y'all live in the same house, I treat all y'all the same. I expect all y'all to act the same." Nothing ever justified our "actin' up or actin' out." If we did, we knew what to expect. Mama was a "right and wrong, good and bad" kind of person, no in-betweens, no situational ethics. Everything was either black or white—no such thing as gray. We always knew where she stood.

Mama also had a faith that never wavered. Each week brought us new and repeated challenges, but at the end of each week Mama took us to church. At church we sat in the same section, closer to the front than back. Three ceiling fans circulated the hot air above, while paper hand fans pushed the hot air below. The long wooden pews were marred with etchings left by bored and distracted children. Lettie and I sat on Mama's right; Henry and Gary sat on her left. The youngest next to her, all within arm's reach.

The part of the service that I hated was the intercessory prayer because it was always conducted on our knees, knees that rested on knotted pine floors, knees that were knotted with pain. As the minister bellowed out thanksgiving, praise, and pleas for forgiveness of sins, I would open my eyes to see Mama's lips moving. Perhaps she had something else to say to God. The frown on her forehead and the wringing of her hands must have meant her prayer was far more important. I became frightened when she slowly shook her head from side to side, as in an attempt to erase an unwanted reality. Daddy's addiction to alcohol was an unwanted reality.

On that day, Mama seemed more troubled than usual, but her eyes stayed on the preacher up front. Our eyes stayed on her. We followed her lead.

The day before, when the shiny, white Chevrolet pulled up to our house, we knew it was Daddy's friend and coworker Mr. Avery. He was the only one we knew who had a nice car. The only time he came was to bring Daddy home when Daddy was too drunk to make it on his own. Before Mr. Avery could stop his car, Daddy had already opened the passenger door. The weight of the door forced Daddy back to his seat. Daddy's clumsy attempt to climb the front steps was made more pronounced by his bowlegs, his sixty extra pounds of weight, and his inebriated swagger. Once Daddy was inside, Mr. Avery knew his friend was safe at home. Mr. Avery also knew of Mama's heartache. Behind closed doors and thin walls, he heard the one-sided argument as Mama fussed, cried, and lambasted Daddy for his drunkenness.

The intercessory prayer was coming to an end, but Mama's anguish was not. Just as the salty sweat from her brow joined the tears from her swollen eyes, one unwanted reality seemed to join hands with another. I mentally blocked out the minister's voice and leaned closer to Mama. I heard an almost inaudible whisper. It wasn't about Daddy. It was something about another baby.

―――――――

It was almost dark. Lettie and I were in forbidden territory. We were at Mosley Park, and night came even faster from that distance. It would most certainly be dark by the time Lettie and I reached home. Mama instructed us to stay close to home, anywhere within the vicinity so that we could easily be found. With no health or life insurance, the last place she needed to find us was in the hospital or the morgue. The farther we ventured from our house, the greater the likelihood that the community residents did not know us. Our antics usually meant incidents—incidents that meant accidents, and accidents that, before the 911 emergency system, could have resulted in one of us dying as a stranger in someone else's front yard.

Mosley Park on Hunter Street was strictly forbidden not only because of its distance but also because of its reputation for danger. Although this was a city park, the deepest end of the swimming pool had a dirt floor. Over time, sticks, bottles, cans, and trash found its way into the pool's bottom. It was seldom cleaned and probably never chlorinated. Despite its green murky waters, black children, especially the adventurous ones, still found it inviting for swimming. There were always fewer swimmers in this section; therefore, lifeguards rarely patrolled this area of the pool. This was not only hazardous for swimmers; it was also problematic for an unescorted child. Mischievous teenagers had been known to target an unattended child who was standing close enough to be pushed in. If this happened late in the evening, sometimes it would be the next day before the body could be seen floating near the surface of the water.

The sound of the glaring jukebox lured us to the concession hall, where we got caught up in the excitement. Before we knew it, it was almost dark. Knowing the fate that awaited us, Lettie came up with a plan. Instead of admitting where we were, we agreed to say that we fell asleep at a neighbor's house. We agreed to stick with this lie no matter what happened. We were interrogated separately, and my story never changed. I didn't know that she reneged on me. Lettie's punishment was short. My punishment was unmerciful because I refused to change my story. When I realized that my punishment lasted longer and was more severe than Lettie's, my stubbornness was pushed to a new height. The beatings failed to subdue me. Instead they only fueled my fury.

❧ AN EVEN DOZEN ❧

I never thought about it before, but with Daddy's job keeping him gone most of the time, Mama was really a single parent. She acted more like a double one. Mama was like an air traffic controller at a major airport. Her focus was on the big jets, not the prop planes. That summer we all learned what happens when a prop plane runs off course. I'm sure everyone in our house had his or her own share of drama and trauma, but I didn't notice anyone else's. I was consumed by my own.

The fact that my older sister still wore an overcoat long into the July heat meant nothing to me. We all did quirky things; this was just another one. But Mama knew what it meant. It meant her daughter was seven months pregnant. Most families eagerly await the birth of the first grandchild, but Mama was still struggling under the weight of the children she had birthed herself. Of course the social stigma made it embarrassing, but perhaps Mama was more saddened by the certain hard times and difficulties that she knew were inevitable for her unwed daughter and this young child.

On September 25, 1959, Myrna Annette was born. At the age of nine, I became an aunt. In the '50s, black folks rarely had anything that was brand new, anything that had not been discards of the white man, anything that was totally and uniquely their own. A new baby, and all that comes with it, was totally ours.

It is hard not to love a new baby, regardless of the circumstances surrounding the birth. Myrna was the cutest thing I had ever seen. She was like a doll, and I couldn't keep my hands or eyes off of her. She had a head full of curly hair and big bright eyes, and she even had light skin! My brothers were more amused than excited. The first time they saw her crawl, it seemed as if she had a motor in her diapers. She could move across the floor at breakneck speed. The funnier thing was that anything that was in her path, she managed to put in her mouth. This child was known to eat anything on the floor and from the garbage. My brothers appropriately gave her the nickname of "Germ." As a toddler, she followed me everywhere and did everything I told her to do. She stuck like glue even when I was purposely mean to her. She was more like a younger sibling, but unlike Henry, she never fought back. As a child she mimicked my every move and adopted my personality and style as her own.

When I went away to school and we no longer played together, we still shared an amazing bond. I later learned that, when we were literally miles apart, she and I had the same life adolescent challenges around the same time, and we resolved them in exactly the same manner. As a young adult, she confided that I was her idol. If I had known she was watching I would have done a lot of things differently.

My entire family embraced Myrna, not as a grandchild, but as one of us. Our family size was rounded out to twelve. We got the even dozen, but I don't think Dr. Mac ever made good on his promise of a free delivery.

1960

Life Lessons

At the age of ten, I became a bully to James Wilson (his real name). Stupidity and naiveté must have been stamped in my DNA because I didn't see this activity as bullying. Only when I decided to write this story did I realize that it was bullying in its purest form. James was a short, slightly built boy who was shy and unassuming. Although I was slight myself, I had a noticeable height advantage. Each day after school I noticed that in order to get home, we traveled a short distance down Andrews Street together, then our paths parted. Andrews Street intersected with Holly Road directly across the street from our school. One of many unpaved roads in the neighborhood, Andrews Street crested about fifty yards from the school, at which point the school was out of sight. Large gravel stones covered the surface, and since James was closer to the ground than anyone else, he appeared to be having difficulty keeping his balance and balancing his books underneath his arm. I then realized that the scenario was the same as with Teresa: we were

Linda Joyce, age ten

69

just out of the sight of authority, I had an advantage over him, and there was an audience. So I just decided to go over to him and see if it worked.

For no other reason than being evil, I pushed him down. He looked up at me in surprise and asked, "What did you do that for?" I didn't answer right away because suddenly a strange rush came over me—a rush of power. When he did not attempt to retaliate, I felt even better. Then I said, "Just because." He then gathered his books and scampered away. You would think that since I had just been on the other end of the stick, I would have empathized with him, but I didn't. By now I had taken my share of unjustified torture and I felt it was time to spread it around.

Each day I could hardly wait for the dismissal bell to ring before I darted across the street to catch up with James. No doubt, he had begun to look for me, just as I had looked for Teresa. As soon as we were out of sight of the school, I began jabbing him in the stomach. He pleaded for me to stop, but of course I didn't. He simply walked backward all the way home, never trying to defend himself. I don't know how long this went on. If you ask him, he'd probably say forever. One day in exasperation he shouted, "Stop it. My mama said that I cannot hit girls!" What? I had never heard anyone say that girls should not be hit. Somebody needed to tell my daddy that. Now instead of me retreating and realizing that this boy was a man in the making, I rationalized that his mama was actually on my side, giving me permission to beat him up. After all, I would be stupid not to, since his mama said he could not defend himself. From then on, my attacks on him were relentless. I became so caught up in the bullying process that I forgot all about the "boiling point and element of surprise" phase. One day when we were barely out of sight from the school, I readied my fist to punch him in the stomach. Before I knew it, I was on the ground.

To this day I don't know what happened, except he must have taken his foot and kicked the back of my knees. Once again, the element of surprise was at work, because I was caught completely off guard. James stood there looking down on me, afraid that he had hurt me but still afraid to come closer to help, just in case. Now the laughter was on me, and I was embarrassed. To this day I have never bullied again. I wonder if Teresa learned the same lesson. Maybe the word had spread around the school about the folding-chair incident because I never heard from Teresa again.

James Wilson, if you are out there and reading this, I ask your forgiveness. I am truly sorry. Teresa, if you are out there reading this, "Try pulling my chair back again."

❧ "WAIT 'TIL YOUR DADDY GETS HOME" ❧

We didn't realize that when Mama stopped whipping us, she began saying, "Wait 'til your Daddy gets home." It took me a minute to notice the changing of the guard. I didn't understand that she was saving my punishment for Daddy to administer.

Mama's announcement of his imminent return began to strike fear in my heart. Those days were the only times that I thought of my body and soul because I knew all too well what would happen to both when Daddy pulled out his razor strap. This was also the only time I ever thought about running away. My sister tried it several times, but where would I go? My poor vision kept me imprisoned to surroundings that were only familiar in daylight. Neighbors sent you home at mealtimes, and child abduction wasn't in vogue in the black community.

I woke early one morning when I knew I had a beating coming, knowing I had to get away. I couldn't just wait for him to come for me. The house was quiet, but I knew he was home. I smelled him. There's no smell like the sickening caustic body odor of a drunkard, one who falls asleep with a whiskey bottle in one hand and a smoldering cigar in the other. The stench of his cigar was a dry irritant in my nose and itchiness in my eyes. It permeated the air and weaved its own threads through the sofa, bed, curtains, and our clothes. It was a sickeningly pungent smell, a strong cord, the likes of which knotted its grip in my mind. One end of his cigar was wet and mashed flat by thick lips that sucked its poison, the other end jagged with white ash. It was a brown log that bore a strong resemblance to the end product of his last meal. The thought of it all made me dizzy. The fear of it made me lightheaded. I had to get out of the house just to breathe.

Mamma and Daddy now slept next door to us, in the first room on the right. It was daybreak but no one was stirring. As I crept past their bedroom door I heard his heavy breathing, interrupted by snorts and snoring.

It was an early spring morning. My first thought was to hide beneath the house, but my legs were now clearly half the length of my body and I could no longer crouch there, much less stand. The sky was clear. The air was still and crisp. The streets were empty and my heart was full. I headed east on Arcadia, the longest street, because that gave me time to think. This street also had more hills and curves, which enabled me to get out of plain sight quickly. I thought I was walking slowly, but before I knew it I had circled the block and was almost back home. I then doubled back and wove between side streets that carried me to Stafford Street. I thought, *I'm tired and hungry. What else do you do when you run away?* The neighborhood began to stir as doors opened to retrieve bottled milk from front porches and newspapers from front lawns. As I turned to walk up Stafford Street once again, Henry used his hands as a megaphone and shouted, "Lin, Daddy is looking for you!" I quickened with fear as I turned and saw the image of Henry at the bottom of the hill. I could not see his face, but I knew he had a big grin on it. He loved delivering this kind of news. I knew from experience that if I did not respond quickly, he would shout louder and longer. In an instant, my eyes filled with tears at the exact time that my bladder filled to overflowing. I twisted my legs to hold back the flow and inched my way back toward our house.

When Daddy had come home last month he beat me. Whenever he came home he beat me. Was that the only reason he came home? When Daddy woke early that morning to deliver me from my demons, someone told him that I had run away. That made him angry. By the age of ten I had an impressive rap sheet: stubborn and lazy, lying and stealing, disobeying and betraying, acting up in school and acting like a fool, talking back, and worse yet, hitting Mama back. That day I added "running away" to that list.

As Daddy unraveled his long leather strap, perhaps he thought, *The nerve of this child, thinking she can run away from me. Where she gon' go? She got to come back sometime. All she doing is wastin' my time. I'll beat the devil out*

of her yet. Bet she won't run away no mo'! I was now only several doors away
from our house. My head was telling me that I was crazy to go willingly to my
executioner, but it could not tell me where else to go. My heart was so full of
fear that I could feel its frantic beat in the back of my eyes, nearsighted eyes so
full of tears that provided no clear direction either way. My swollen bladder
burned to be relieved. I twisted my knock-kneed skinny legs tight enough to
hold back the flow, but I kept them loose enough to keep me mobile. Any
onlooker would think I had been born with a deformity.

I cut across the neighbor's backyard and entered the house through the
back door. The back door was closest to the bathroom and farthest away
from Daddy's room. The bathroom, a small enclosure off the kitchen, had a
low toilet, a small sink, no medicine cabinet or mirror, a bathtub almost as
low as the toilet, a small window, and a small roll of toilet paper on the floor.
Everything in that room was small, including me. My panties were already
damp, either from perspiration or pee, probably both. I sat down anyway,
waiting for my entire being to come together in one space. The next sound that
I heard was, "Linda Joyce, get in here!" Mama was the only one who called me
"Linda Joyce," but that command didn't come from Mama. It was Daddy. He
was tired of waiting. I rushed to the opened door of the second room on the
right to let him know I was no longer stalling. As I stepped inside its threshold,
my body froze as if captured in a picture frame.

There Daddy sat on the side of the bed. He had changed. He appeared sick.
He seemed swollen, much larger than before. His massive weight prevented
him closing his legs and sitting up straight. He seemed tired, not up to the
task but determined to do it anyway. This morning, he knew he was not about
to chase me around the neighborhood. His physical condition let him know
he could no longer chase me around the room. This was perhaps the reason
he locked my head in his knees. Perhaps this was also a symbolic gesture that
meant my mind should be gripped by fear of him.

The air inside the room was thicker than anywhere else in the house. His
sweat and my sweat, a urine-soaked mattress, and my damp underwear made
the air stink. Both of us were crazed animals: he was the hunter; I was the

hunted. My older sister and younger brothers huddled in a corner. Henry was no longer grinning.

I don't remember disrobing, but I do remember the cool breeze from the open window that fanned my shameful nakedness. I don't remember dropping to my knees, and I don't remember how long it took to get me into his headlock grip, but I do remember his knees clamping out the sound in my ears and my eyes seeing only darkness and dust beneath my bed. As the downward stroke of the leather strap cut the air above, simultaneously the fire that radiated from my butt illuminated the darkness beneath the bed. Any subsequent blows went unnoticed because my brain didn't have time to synthesize the pain. In the midst of my agonizing screams I heard the muffled plea of Mama saying, "Melvin, you're beating her too hard!" Much later my sister told me there was a strange look on Daddy's face when Mama begged him to stop. Perhaps he thought, *You always complainin' 'bout me not doing nothing right. Now the one thing I know how to do right, now you complain 'bout that.*

I don't know how many times he hit me, but perhaps the final blow of his strap was out of frustration for his inability to control me and his inability to please Mama, because he said, "And you got the nerve to hit yo' mama back?" Blood trickled down my outer thigh as he released his headlock. Snot and tears covered my face as my limp body fell to the floor. He gave me a final dare and said, "Now hit me back!" He waited for my response. He hesitated a bit longer, just in case I was stuck on stupid. I didn't take the dare. He left the room. The tension-filled room was now still. All that could be heard were moaning, sobs, and heavy breathing—mine. Everyone else had left the room. I was left on the cold wooden floor, beside the bed. I cried blood. I bled tears. I tasted hate, a taste that lasted for forty years.

Later that day Mama came to my room to check on me. My head was turned to the wall. I couldn't see her, but I felt her presence. She didn't come close, just close enough to be certain I was still breathing. She threw out another one of her sayings: "When you find yourself in a hole, stop digging."

❧ THE FACTS OF LIFE ❧

Although Mama had brought eleven children into this world, she could never bring herself to talk to us about the facts of life. The most she told us girls was, "Keep your legs closed and your dress down." She would have to amend that advice today since almost everyone wears pants. The other relationship advice that she gave freely and often was, "It's a stupid woman who sleeps with a man who beats her." Domestic violence was no doubt a part of her culture because she said, "Some women are like a jack-in-the-box 'cause all you gotta do is knock 'em in the head and their legs fly open." She said, "A man may catch you off guard the first time but he has to go to sleep sometimes. That's when you catch him off guard." I don't recall Mama ever giving the boys any training that men should never hit women, at least no straightforward or cut-to-the-chase sayings like she gave us girls. Many women supporters and sympathizers today would say that Mama's statements about women were too harsh. They'd argue that some women are weak; some feel trapped with nowhere to go. Toward the end of Mama's life, she did become more flexible in her thinking. If she were alive today, I'm sure she would revise her advice somewhat. She probably would say, "Any woman who sleeps with a man who beats her is a weak, trapped, and stupid woman with nowhere to go."

Jokingly I asked her if she put that curious-looking knot on Daddy's head and if he had ever hit her. The indignant expression on her face spoke louder than words when she said, "If he had beat me, there sho' wouldn't be eleven of y'all. That's one thing me and yo' daddy don't do. We do not pass licks!"

❧ HOW NOT TO PICK YOUR MATE ❧

Mama once told me of a love story that had a tragic end. Although life was hard for blacks in the late 1920s, falling in love had a way of making a hard life worth living. In the South, young girls carried ice picks in their purses, much like young guys carried pocketknives in their pockets.

If a young suitor offered to buy a sassafras tea or soda water for a young lady, she could reciprocate by chipping small pieces of ice to cool the drink. If the young girl was more aggressive, it was a common practice simply to nick the guy with the ice pick, ever so gently, just to get his attention. One day a young lady became overzealous and nicked a guy too hard in the wrong place. She punctured his lung and killed him.

The entire black community was doubly distraught because one young life ended quickly by accident and the other life would end slowly behind prison bars. The young lady was devastated by depression and remorse, so much so that the victim's family joined efforts with her family to harbor her in hiding for twenty years. For obvious reasons, black-on-black crimes were not aggressively pursued. The legal system didn't care what black folks did, as long as they did it to each other.

Twenty years later when the police found her, she was mentally unstable and looked crazed. She was sickly and had picked her head clean of nearly every strand of hair. When the judicial system evaluated her mental condition and the circumstances around the tragedy, all charges were dropped.

1961

Guidepost

If our family had one stable force, one guidepost during that time, it was Mama. There was always calamity at her feet, chaos at hand, and confusion all around, but she held her head high, directing us through the storms.

Mama was one of many unseen black women in the South who worked all their lives, didn't end up on welfare, stayed married because that's what God-fearing people of her generation did (whether they were happy or not), and managed not to get strung out on drugs, whiskey, or a cast of nameless, no-account men. I wanted to be someone different from Mama, but in some ways I wanted to be just like her.

❧ MY STRUGGLE FOR ACCEPTANCE ❧

My early experiences on Arcadia Circle were actually the planks in the rickety bridge that carried me into adolescence. I consciously and subconsciously tried to find clarity. Going through my preteens was a painful and awkward experience. When I was younger, if I did something immature, I heard, "You're old enough to know better."

As a preteen, if I took the initiative to do something, I heard, "You must think you're grown." If I asked a question, the answer was either one that I should have known or something that was none of my business. Amid all the craziness I couldn't fit in at home. Now I tried in earnest to fit in at school. By now I was probably a handful for my teachers and I had proven their assumptions that I had little potential to amount to anything.

One day at school, I sat back and observed the girls whom I envied. I quickly learned that they were lazy and cared less about learning and more about looks. Of course good grades helped their social standing, but looks carried more weight. I surmised that if I did my homework and let the light-skinned girls copy from my paper, they would be my friends. Little did I know at the time that this was not true friendship. I wanted to be included so badly that I figured that this was a small price to pay.

The more I read, the more I learned. Each night I worked diligently to complete assignments to perfection, only for the other girls to get the credit. All of our grades improved. Soon I wanted to learn everything I could. Once I knew I had it, I thirsted for more. Back in class when the teachers asked a question, my hand was the first to go up. I surprised my classmates, my teachers, and myself. My grades improved and so did my conduct. When I got an A at the end of a grading period, Mama was pleased and she gave me a dime. I liked pleasing Mama. That school year was my best. It was also the first of more good years to come. Little did I realize that I was developing good study habits that would serve me well going forward.

My physical appearance changed drastically but not for the better. Although I was still nearly blind, I sensed that my legs were now half the length of my body. I thought my arms were too long, my shoulders too broad, my nose too wide, my lips too thick, and of course my skin too dark. I was thin, and I looked malnourished. Even my dimples disappeared. My poor self-image consumed my thinking. But at least my hair had begun to grow. Now I was able to make two pigtails that I could secure with rubber bands.

❧ MORE ANTICS FROM HENRY ❧

I remember a time when Henry taunted me and I brandished a pair of rusty scissors to defend myself. He quickly grabbed my hand and turned the scissors in my direction. Once again, stubbornness and stupidity prevented me from dropping the scissors. Before I knew it, the scissors punctured my left upper thigh, just one inch below my birthmark. Henry's eyes became big as saucers at the sight of blood gushing out of my gaping wound. I screamed, more out of fear than pain. When Mama came home I was taken to the small community clinic, where Dr. McLendon was on staff. After my injury was treated, Dr. Mac questioned me as to how the incident happened. I told him that my brother was teasing me with scissors and accidentally stabbed me (except I conveniently left out the part that the scissors were actually in my hands at the time). During the entire procedure he questioned me repeatedly about the incident and my story never wavered.

After he finished the third stitch and applied the bandage, Dr. Mac looked me directly in the eye and said, "Your brother was trying to rape you, wasn't he?" I was stunned and could not reply. I think my silence confirmed his flawed suspicion. I never told anyone about my culpability in the incident nor did I ever tell of the doctor's suspicion.

Over the years, my birthmark has become less recognizable than the scissor scar below it. Today, that scar is a constant reminder that Doctor Mac had treated similar wounds that left much deeper scars than mine. This was confusing because when I was younger and defenseless, an adult thought I fabricated an alleged sexual assault. Now that I was older and able to fend for myself, an adult was trying to persuade me to admit to a sexual aggression that did not happen.

Henry's antics persisted long into his adolescent years, but they became more clandestine. By the time we found out, his silly tricks were planned and well-honed. Not only was he mischievous, he was equally inquisitive. He took apart everything he touched, wanting to see why and how things worked. He spent many hours alone tinkering with discarded radios, transistors, batteries, motors, and anything that powered something else or was powered by something else. None of us knew it, but Henry was actually an avid tactile learner who was mastering physics and mechanical engineering at an early age.

Henry's first tryst with the law came when he was about thirteen, a minor offense that only required him and Mama to appear in court and pay a fine. Decades later his brushes with the law were more daring and costly.

—————

The temperature outside was a balmy 101 degrees, much too hot for an August evening in Atlanta. The steady hum of the air conditioner guaranteed a cooler temperature inside, and the smell of hot fried fish guaranteed some good eating was about to take place.

The combination kitchen/dining area was the usual gathering place for most of the activity in Melvin's house, maybe because most of the activity involved eating. One evening just before dinner, the telephone rang. The caller said, "Man, turn to Channel 2. You got to see this. A dude is leading a high-speed chase downtown!" The six o'clock news had started five minutes earlier, and my brother Melvin had purposely turned off the television. There was no end to the types of things that aired on the evening news in a city as diverse as Atlanta. Nothing surprised him anymore, so nothing was new.

"Man, I'm trying to eat my dinner. I don't have time for the crap on Channel 2," was Melvin's reply. High-speed chases were common. Melvin had seen many of those, but this dude must have been some kind of fool to think he could get away with that. The caller breathlessly relayed every detail of the chase as Melvin turned on the TV. He didn't have to check channels because now all channels were giving live coverage of the interstate drama.

The escaping car was traveling so fast that it was difficult to discern its color, make, or model. Suddenly the car stopped and shots rang out. Melvin thought this scene was straight out of the movies. When the revolver was empty the assailant threw out his gun, and a barrage of police officers rushed in to take him into custody. Although the renegade had surrendered and was unarmed, several police officers began beating him severely with billy clubs. He was then handcuffed and thrown into a police van and taken to jail. The news reporter's camera angle failed to give the viewing audience a good picture of the man's identity. Melvin said the cops' billy clubs left the man's head looking like peanut brittle.

Of course that story was the next morning's headlines. Only after reading the full details of the event did Melvin come to know that the fool was our brother Henry. Later Henry told us that he was only taking back what was his in the first place. He said the gun just happened to be under the seat of the stolen tow truck and that he was not trying to hurt anyone. He was just trying to keep the cops from hurting him. Henry had clearly developed a prison mentality, and all of our reasoning was useless. This escapade would be one of many that would chronicle his lifelong affair with the Georgia Correctional System.

1962

Desegregation

In the early 1960s there was segregation in almost everything, including schools. Schools were supposedly separate but equal, which of course was untrue. All white schools flourished with books and equipment whereas black schools had almost nothing. The few books we had, we shared in school. We took turns taking books home, and I'll give you three guesses as to what happened when I managed to take a book home. If I were lucky enough to get a book to take home, that day's assignment was on a page that had been ripped out. If you took a book home, you were still expected to turn in homework even though there was no page in the textbook. The school library was used once a month as a fallout shelter test site for emergency air raids and was only opened during school hours. Students were only allowed entrance as an entire class unit. The public library was my only option.

In 1955 the U.S. Supreme Court said that segregation of city facilities was unconstitutional but the Atlanta library defied court orders and denied petitions to desegregate. The public libraries on the black side of town were ill-equipped, much like the schools. But that was all we had, all that we knew. Ours was located two miles away on Morris Brown Drive. I had been there before, and I knew from experience that my trip required planning. I had to get mentally psyched for the journey. There were no crosswalks or sidewalks.

I knew how to navigate the streets where stray dogs roamed. I knew the yards where I had twisted my spindly ankles in hidden potholes. I would come across several busy intersections along the way but only one traffic light. My impaired vision added to my anxiety because speeding cars rounding blind curves could not see me, and I could not see them.

Once inside the library my challenges began anew. I had to learn the Dewey Decimal System. This system, developed by Melvil Dewey, organized books on library shelves in a specific and repeatable order. That made it easy to find any book and return it to its proper place. Although Dewey tried to make it easy, nothing is easy when your sight is impaired. Navigating the heavy wooden card catalog required time and patience. If someone was using the drawer I wanted, I had to wait. When it became available, I had to take the entire drawer out of the cabinet, over to a table. I literally had to place the cards on my nose in order to read the fine print. After returning the heavy drawer to the rack, I had to stand close to each book on the shelf in order to match the call numbers with my reference. Most of the time the books were out of place or had been checked out. This required another search of the card catalog. Years before Daylight Savings Time came into play, Atlanta city streets became dark quickly at night in the winter months.

My poor eyesight made any time after dusk problematic. The lone traffic light in front of the library provided the only safe crossing. The remainder of my journey became even more perilous due to the weak-voltage streetlights placed only on corners. The scariest part was walking beneath a train trestle on Hunter Street near Pilgrims Travelers' Church. The oncoming cars were so close that the passing current swirled my dress above my head. By the time I made it safely back home, all the dinner was gone. In order to be fed, you had to be there when the food came off the stove. Once Mama prepared a meal, she didn't have time to stand guard and ration. The main thing we had to learn about any meal at our house was "survival of the fittest." Sometimes I was one of the fittest. That day I was not.

———————

Something was always going on between Henry and me.

It was a setup, another time when Henry's antics and roughhousing caused me pain. I ran into the house rubbing the swollen lump over my left eye. Henry followed close behind, anxious to own up to being devilish. Adding a little drama for special effect, I screamed, "Mama, Henry hit me in the head with a rock!" With her knuckles raised and ready for reprimand, Mama said, "Boy, didn't I tell you not to throw rocks?" By the age of ten Henry had already mastered the art of doing wrong in such a way as to avoid punishment. Henry's grin had already widened eagerly to reply, "That was not a rock. That was one of her biscuits!"

❧ EXTRA CASH ❧

Mama was busy stretching lace curtains on the blocking frames. The frames had small pins around the edges for attaching the lace. Mama was tired, and she kept pricking her fingers and staining the margins with her blood. Assembly of this frame usually required enlisting the man of the house to set up the curtain stretchers for the exact measurements of the curtains. No one had basements for the curtains to dry, so the stretchers were set up in the backyard.

Those were the days of curtain stretchers and Argo starch. In addition to daily cleaning at Mrs. Peterson's house, a day was set aside for polishing silver, waxing furniture, and stretching lace curtains. At a time when black folks struggled to stretch a dollar to feed their families, white folks were making a big deal over starching and stretching lace curtains.

Wednesday was curtain-stretching day for Mrs. Peterson's house, but not at her house. Instead it was at ours. Mrs. Peterson was not the type of white woman who would ever allow such contraptions in her yard. So Mama brought them home and stretched them in our backyard. She was still working for that woman at our house, with no extra pay! Mama didn't like doing the white folks' work at our home, especially when there was always so much of her own work to be done. But Mama knew she had to please the white folks if she wanted to keep her job. When neighbors came by and saw how skilled she was at this cumbersome task, they offered to pay her to stretch their curtains, doilies, and tablecloths.

Mama had become an expert at stretching a dollar, now she learned how to stretch the leftover starch from Mrs. Peterson's job. Already working two full-time jobs, it wasn't long before Mama was busy working another steady part-time job as well. I never could have guessed that stretching lace curtains would possibly gain me favor with one of the meanest teachers in the Atlanta Public School system.

By the seventh grade I had begun to settle down. When I drew praise and recognition for my schoolwork, my conduct followed a straighter path. I was doing well in school, much better than my teachers had expected. One of my teachers, Mrs. Thelma Branch, was a guidepost along that path. Although she was fair-skinned she was also very fair in the way she treated each student. Scholastic performance was far more important than skin color, the length of your hair, or who your parents were.

Mrs. Branch had an accent and an attitude that let us know she was not from Atlanta, not from anywhere in Georgia, and as far as we could tell not from the United States. She enunciated her words as if she were reading a Shakespeare play. The other indication that she was not one of us was that she found our everyday adolescent antics to be absolutely deplorable. The other teachers seemed to take our silliness in stride. Whenever someone acted out or acted up, Mrs. Branch scolded us and said, "You must have been born in a barn!" The guilty "barn animal" was highly embarrassed when the class broke out in laughter. Since no one liked being described as the class jackass, it wasn't long before each student fell in line (at least in her classroom).

Mrs. Branch decided to harness our unbridled energy and hold auditions for a school play. In retrospect Mrs. Branch was years ahead of her time, because the gist of the play was about embracing diversity. She wanted to teach us how not to judge people by their outward appearance and circumstance. The main character of the play was an alien, much like the modern-day ET, who came to earth and no one wanted him around. When interested students volunteered for character assignments, no one wanted to be known as someone from outer space. Months went by, and no one came forward to play the part of the alien. If Mrs. Branch didn't get casting completed soon, she wouldn't be able to make a spring production deadline. Without the main character, the show could not go on.

My conduct had improved, and Mrs. Branch was no longer calling me a barn animal. I timidly approached her and asked for the alien role. Mrs. Branch was taken aback by my request and did not immediately respond. Her hesitancy was not because she didn't think I could play the character; it was more because the part was lengthy, and because the character was an alien, the plot was woven in a lot of crazy twists and turns. Furthermore, the fast-approaching production date left little time for me to learn my lines. Before she could express her reservations about my request, I threw out an urgent plea, "Please let me try." She immediately responded, "You've got the part." I didn't even have to audition. For the next several months I was consumed in learning my part. I also had to keep pace with my other school assignments so that I could keep my grades up and keep my artificial friends.

This alien character had a name that was a combination of about thirteen letters and numbers: 3K28P61H66DCL. Every time the alien spoke, he repeated his name. And in keeping with what most people think aliens are prone to do, I had to talk fast.

Each evening, back in my bedroom, I practiced my lines and gestures. The same clothes hanging on the back of the door that once appeared as ghosts in my dreams now served as fellow cast members. Late at night, long after the lights were out, my brothers could hear me beneath the covers, practicing my name, 3K28P61H66DCL, and they thought I was crazy.

Each week during rehearsals the other cast members were amazed at how I had mastered my role. Every time I said my name, they forgot their part. Although no one still wanted to be called an alien, they were glad to know one personally. My popularity soared. About three weeks before the scheduled production, Mrs. Branch informed me that I needed to buy an alien costume. What? I had no money, and Mama certainly did not have any. Even if I had saved my lunch money for the entire year, I would only have about nine dollars. I didn't know where to find an alien costume. I didn't know how much one cost. I didn't even know what one looked like, but Mrs. Branch was adamant that I get one. No costume, no production—it was just that simple.

Had I learned these lines for nothing? Had I taken on the shame of being an alien only to take on the embarrassment of causing the entire play to flop? This is where my stubbornness resurfaced again. I immediately began collecting empty soda bottles and returning them for the five-cent deposit. I begged money from older siblings and their friends, from anybody I could. Two weeks before production I had about three dollars, but I still didn't know where to find an alien costume. Amid all the chaos, I failed to consider probably the most crucial issue of all: How was I going to get to the play, and who was going to take me? The production was scheduled on a school night at eight o'clock (well after nightfall). Daddy was not even a remote solution, for obvious reasons. Mama would have just finished working eight hours of daytime labor and would be fast asleep preparing for another eight hours of nighttime labor. My older siblings were no longer required to be at my beck and call. Ten days before production I rushed to the privacy of my bed. The lights were out; the house was quiet. Beneath the covers, you no longer heard the sound of "3K28P61H66DCL" but instead the whimpering tears of a fallen star.

The next morning I arose with a fighting spirit to be in that play, whatever the cost. I approached Mama and begged her to escort me to that play. I already knew her objections, so I promised to clean, cook, iron clothes, and do whatever she normally would be doing in the evenings so she could get some sleep, take me to the play, get home about nine-thirty in the evening, and still have enough time to get to her night job at eleven o'clock that evening. She felt my desperation, she understood my dilemma, and she was proud of what I wanted to do. She said yes!

One week away from production, I was no closer to finding anything that resembled an alien outfit. I had scoured the local five-and-dime store several times, and there were limited other stores within walking distance of my house. This was the year that footed pajamas hit the fashion scene. All of the

Christmas and winter items were now on sale, and I had just enough money to purchase a baby-blue pajama set. The next day I informed Mrs. Branch that I had my costume, I knew my lines, and that I'd be on time for the play.

On the night of the play, Mama and I arrived at the school auditorium. I was especially anxious to get Mrs. Branch's approval on my costume, when suddenly she gasped, "What? You don't look like an alien!" I was crushed. Nonetheless it was thirty minutes away from the opening scene, the audience was full, and the show had to go on. I instructed Mama on where to sit so that she could see me and I could also sneak a peek at her, just to get random approval ratings on how I was doing. Midway through the play, I made my grand entrance. A few people laughed when they saw my costume, but when I rattled off my name, "3K28P61H66DCL," the audience roared! Just as the laughter settled, the script required that I say my name again, and every time that I spoke. Once again, laughter filled the room. This went on throughout the entire play. The audience's approval swelled my head and I was in rare form. I stole the show! At curtain call my performance brought everyone to their feet with applause, and many rushed to the stage to congratulate me. I was so caught up in the excitement that not once had I checked for Mama's approval. I twisted from left to right thanking patrons who were now flanking me on all sides. Surely Mama was somewhere in the throng of people pressing their way to me on stage. Through an opening in the crowd I noticed Mama in her seat, head bowed and fast asleep.

At 9:15 p.m., as we began our walk back home, of course Mama told me that I did well. My mind was still back on stage with 3K28P61H66DCL. Mama's mind was already on the long night ahead. That night, in the second room on the right, the ceiling light flickered from above and a shining star slept below.

❧ FORWARD THINKING ❧

Our house, void of window screens, was easy to spot because dingy curtains flapped wildly outside of double-hung windows. Inside my bedroom a slight film of dust had already covered the sill beneath the window. My sister and brother had begun the family ritual of fanning flies with a towel. Now I had the entire summer to psyche myself up for the unknowns ahead in high school.

While settling on the bed, I heard the end of a radio advertisement that offered something free. Just by sending a written request, anyone could receive a pamphlet about Georgia history. All I needed to do was sell two pop bottles to buy a postage stamp. Within the next twenty-four hours I mailed my request and checked the mailbox daily. Within the next two weeks a brown envelope bearing my name arrived in the mail. I was ecstatic! During the following month, I memorized the name of every county, the state capital, the flower, the bird, the state song, the names of past governors and mayors, and everything related to the state. The summer flew by quickly as the source of my newfound information consumed my every waking minute.

In the early '60s, there was no such thing as a middle school. Elementary school went from kindergarten to seventh grade. High school went from eight through the twelfth grades. In high school there was no orientation to introduce you to the new rules and responsibilities—no preparation for the fast-paced atmosphere of homeroom teacher, student lockers, hall passes, and changing classes.

To my surprise I had unknowingly prepared myself for my eighth-grade civics class. By memorizing all of the information about Georgia, I had an edge over my classmates. I got an A, and I didn't even have to study. At that point I realized that if I studied just a little bit more and a little bit longer, I could be just as smart as anyone else.

Pivotal

❧ THE CEILING LIGHT ❧

A ceiling light hung high above and cast shadows below. Two stress cracks framed its base, a base that held a pull string—knotted twice from previous breaks. The light flickered from dim to bright, but I never knew why, when it would happen, or for how long it would last. Most people look to a Higher Power to give them light, direction, and purpose. Many are lost when that light flickers to darkness.

I never was really knowledgeable about the marches, the sit-ins, the demonstrations, and the entire civil rights era. I don't even remember our church openly praying for Dr. King's safety and success, even though we all benefited from his efforts. Since many of the marches and demonstrations were held on Saturday (the Sabbath), as Seventh-Day Adventists we had a legitimate excuse not to participate. We got a lot of mileage from the phrase, "Be ye in this world but not of the world."

I remember the major headlines about the marches, fire hoses, and dogs. One of those events coincided with a Missionary Volunteer (MV) meeting where the discussion was about heaven. MV was a less formal worship service that was conducted by and for Adventist youths. The meetings were always held on Saturday evenings, prior to sunset. The format was usually a skit, an

open discussion, a sing-along, or a combination of all three. The topic for the
evening was, "What must I do to be saved?" Everyone readily agreed that, first,
all of the Ten Commandments had to be obeyed. Someone added, "So that
means that anyone who does not keep the Sabbath cannot go to heaven." I had
attended this church since birth, but I had not joined as an official member
yet. By now, all of the church's doctrines, practices and ideology were so
ingrained in me that I accepted everything and questioned nothing, but that
last statement about "only Sabbath-keepers being allowed into heaven" didn't
sit well with me and I had to speak up. I sprang from my seat and said, "Wait
a minute. Do you mean to tell me that since Martin Luther King Jr. doesn't
worship on Saturday, he can't go to heaven?" A silence and stillness fell on the
audience. In that stillness I realized I had never heard Dr. King's name spoken
from the pulpit. The silence was now becoming awkward, but no one seemed
able to end it. Finally someone said, "God will not hold you responsible for
what you do not know. If Dr. King doesn't know about the Sabbath, he will not
be held accountable." I quickly responded, "Wait a minute. Dr. King is not an
idiot. He is well-read and probably more educated than anyone in this entire
city. Surely he is reading the same Bible as you and I."

The silence that followed mixed with angst from the church elders. I had
opened a can of worms that no one could put back in the can. A minister in
the audience came forth and took charge of the service. He quoted several
scriptures from the Bible and then several quotes from Ellen G. White's
The Desire of Ages. Absolutely *none* of what he said related to the discussion
and certainly did not answer my question. When the minister finished his
scriptures, someone gave the benediction and the open discussion was closed.
That was the first of many instances when I witnessed that the Bible, which
was supposed to be a vehicle to unite people, was also a source of a great divide.

Perhaps going to church while Daddy was alive provided more of a diversion
than any direction. For the first thirteen years of my life I felt invisible in that
religious experience. I did whatever Mama did.

In the early '60s a powerful evangelist by the name of H. L. Cleveland came
to Atlanta and set the city on fire preaching the gospel and warning everyone

of the soon second coming of Christ. Every world and national event was declared a prophesied sign of the Christ child's return. Each summer a month long tent revival drew large crowds and created traffic jams. Little Richard, the "Tutti Frutti" rock-and-roll star, was a new Adventist convert that year. When he gave his conversion story at one of H. L. Cleveland's tent revivals, hundreds were converted to Adventism in one day. I was one of them. Now religion was no longer a diversion; instead it was a vehicle for deliverance. Mama believed that if she kept us in the church and out of the world, she could also keep us out of harm's way. The next morning's newspaper told her otherwise.

> On Sunday, September 15, 1963, a white man was seen getting out of a white and turquoise Chevrolet car and placing a box under the steps of the 16th Street Baptist Church in Birmingham, Alabama. Soon afterwards, at 10:22 a.m., the bomb exploded killing four girls.

Mama believed that if teachers could deliver us from ignorance, surely religion could deliver us from ignorant white people. The Adventist Church strictly adhered to all of the Ten Commandments, especially those that could be backed by other biblical scriptures. Mama thought that even if this community could not protect us from the evils out there in the world, surely it could save the last four of us from going to hell.

Life at Booker T. Washington High was probably very typical of other black high schools of that day. This huge historic building had four floors. Each hall was lined with broken lockers on one end and broken water fountains and restrooms with stopped-up toilets on the other. About forty classrooms were on each floor. The stairwells were narrow with many broken steps. The graffiti on the stair walls offered random scripts of "who loved whom" and "what teacher ain't shit." The bathroom walls were scripted with more of the same and other four-letter words. The stairwells were the scenes of daily traffic jams when we changed classes and attempted mad dashes to lockers on one end of the hall and bathrooms on the opposite end. In the midst of these noisy, sweaty, musty, tension-filled gridlocks, girls were fondled, pockets were picked, books were lost, and lunches were trampled. I always felt trapped and helpless. It was a small wonder that we were ever in a learning state of mind when we reached our destination.

The classrooms were overcrowded with no air conditioning. The steady hum of a floor fan, circulating hot air, required the teacher to shout in order to be heard. Many students came to school hungry, tired, and troubled. Some were physically and sexually abused. I don't know what our percentage of the school's graduates went on to college, but I'm sure the dropout rate was higher.

In retrospect I think that all of our teachers were dedicated and did their best. Many times their dedication was no match for the casualties of the inner-city struggle. For the most part, the instruction was rote; teacher gave it to the student, and the student gave it back the same way. There was no time for individualism, no time for a different interpretation, no time for letting our imaginations soar, and little time for experimentation and creativity. We had to play catch-up.

❧ PIVOTAL ❧

In 1963 the word "pivotal" was not even a part of my vocabulary. I was still trying to process "reality." How I had processed all of the crazy stuff thus far would set a platform for all of the crazier stuff down the line. Once again I did not realize how deprived I was socially and culturally. I was almost a year older than most of my classmates, but I was easily light-years behind them socially.

It was a Friday afternoon and the weather was a perfect Indian summer in Atlanta. Shortly before 1:30 p.m., a teacher burst into our classroom and shouted, "Everyone put your head on your desk and do not say a word." This was a command that we were used to hearing when we were in the lower grades. We heard it only when we were rowdy. At that time we were not. As she went down the hall I heard her closing each door and giving the same instruction. Something bad had happened.

Our school had an intercom system. Inside of each classroom, centered above the blackboard, was a square brown box with a mesh wire and cloth face.

Every morning the principal's voice came through this contraption to bellow out administrative instructions, announcements, and updates. Whatever had happened, we wondered why he hadn't announced it this morning. Moments later the intercom crackled, the usual indication that an announcement was about to begin. This also gave us unspoken permission to raise our heads. The principal's voice, very stern but unemotional, announced, "The president of the United States, John Fitzgerald Kennedy, has just been assassinated." As I looked around the classroom, the expression on each and every face was that of a blank canvas. Within seconds I could see several canvases flash with "president." Others began to clarify with "President John Fitzgerald Kennedy." Still others illuminated with "President John Fitzgerald Kennedy assassinated."

My poor little canvas flickered only with "assassinated." What in the world was "assassinated"? The only time I ever heard that word was when we read about Abraham Lincoln being killed. That was a million years ago when people were not civilized. We're civilized now, so that can't happen today!

Death was still foreign to me. No one in my immediate family had died, not even a pet because we never had one. I don't recall having attended a funeral. I had a lot to process. For the remainder of the day no one was required to do any schoolwork. The students just sat idle while teachers went from room to room, exchanging information in hushed voices. It was a long day.

When released from school at the end of the day, we burst through the double doors and bled into the streets. Nothing had changed in our world. We were happy to be out of school and back in the streets and backyards of our neighborhoods playing hide-and-seek, hopscotch, or dodgeball. Most of us had televisions at that time. We had one, but with more than twenty-four hands constantly manipulating the controls, the knobs no longer worked. Our television could only be powered on with a can opener. Over time, almost everyone's antenna got better reception with aluminum foil. The evening news probably had word about the assassination, but that was the news channel we avoided.

The next morning, the newspapers were filled with tributes, testimonials, and reflective essays honoring America's favorite son.

I always saw white people as happy and in control. The only time I saw them act negatively or irrationally was when it came to how they treated black folks. Now it was another white person—Lee Harvey Oswald—who angered them, who turned their world upside down, who made them drop to their knees. For the next thirty days, white folks' anger was not outwardly aimed at blacks but toward one of their own. Black America mourned with the rest of the world, even amid strong racial unrest and injustices.

The nation was gripped in sorrow, but I was gripped in fear because of the sorrow. The newspaper and television were filled with scenes of white women and men falling into the streets crying and screaming. Everyone was visibly shaken and traumatized to the core as if they had encountered something they could not handle.

To this point in my life, I had never seen a white person cry. Remember that I had never been in the presence of white people, except on their terms, on their time, and definitely only when they could present themselves in the very best of circumstances. What did white people have to cry about? It was their world. They had everything and controlled everything. The most I had known of white people crying was when I read my textbooks that said, "See Jane fall down. Jane cried boo-hoo boo-hoo." I actually thought that was how white people cried. If the white people's world was coming to an end, what would happen to mine? I was never consumed in the events surrounding the assassination as much as I was frightened by seeing white people grieve. The reality that we were not yet civilized and that John F. Kennedy had met the same fate as Abraham Lincoln began to set in. For the next several months, life was not "business as usual." While the remainder of the free world was searching for answers, the clan at 97 Arcadia Circle was searching for its next meal.

The shiny white Chevrolet pulled up to our house again. We knew it was Mr. Avery bringing Daddy home. The car had idled for several minutes, and no one had opened a door. Finally Mr. Avery emerged and walked around to the passenger side of his car. Daddy was too wasted to walk. Mr. Avery opened the door, lifted and flung Daddy's arm over his shoulder. When he got Daddy inside, Mama was there, waiting with tears in her eyes. She saw two men who went off to work to provide for their families. Two came back, one carrying the other. One was neat, clean, and sober. The other was smelly, soused, and slovenly. Mr. Avery knew what she was up against and asked how he could help. Mama's only reply was, "Can you make him do better?" There were many things Mr. Avery could do, but that was not one of them.

1964

The Highs and Lows of High School

I was in the ninth grade when I had my first run-in with my French teacher, Miss Carter. Miss Carter was in her early twenties, fresh out of college. I suspect that her beginnings were much like mine. In an attempt to look professional and separate herself from the students, each day she wore a different color plastic headband that matched one color in her dress. Regardless of the color of her dress and headband, she always wore the same black patent-leather shoes. She was probably the first in her family to finish college. She indeed had something to be proud of. Now that she had become a teacher, she also obviously had something to prove.

At the age of fourteen, I saw no need for learning a foreign language that I would certainly never use. I took the class only because I had to. My plan was to just show up, go to sleep, and get a D. If I could get an A in physical education, that would balance my average up to a C. It was an unspoken rule. It was simple as that. Miss Carter had different plans. She knew the unspoken rules also, and she was going to rewrite them in her class. She graded on the curve, the downward curve. Our personalities clashed immediately. She woke me up one day and shouted out in class, "If you think you will get out of my class with a D, you have another thought coming." She assured me that I would most certainly get an F for sleeping in her class. In retrospect, that may have been her way of motivating me, but I took it as a threat. I mumbled under my breath, "Oh no, not today, sister. You'll never flunk me! I'll show you." The war was on.

I practiced my French while playing hopscotch, and I rolled my tongue in defiance: *Très bien, très bien.* I practiced while washing dishes, and as I scrubbed a pot I learned to emphasize the last syllable more than the others: Bon*jour*, ma*dame*, mer*ci*. I practiced while taking a bath and perfected the nasal sound of "O" words: *orange, ordinaire.* I was on a roll. I thought, *Piece of cake. I can do this.* By the end of the semester, my borderline D had changed to a C. I swear I think the teacher resented me for proving her wrong.

Next semester we started conjugating verbs. I talked to myself each night, "Remember, Linda, this stuff isn't spelled like it sounds, and you got to do your mouth funny so it can sound right. Miss Carter has a mouth full of crooked teeth. She was made to speak this language. Not me. Try again." I drilled myself for hours on end.

Back in class the teacher said, "Je suis," and I replied, "Tu es." She gave it to me; I gave it back to her. I went home the next night and got even better.

Practice, practice, practice. Before I knew it, I was a fifteen-year-old French-verb-conjugating fool. Back in class, Miss Carter fired the question at me. I fired the answer back at her. Each day, she ignored the other students and went straight for my jugular vein. She targeted me, and I defended each blow. It was as if she had a personal vendetta to trip me up, to catch me off guard, to flunk me. I was too stubborn to let her win. It wasn't long before she eased up and said, "I guess you can learn something after all." I didn't comment openly, but my ego was having a Fourth of July celebration inside.

My final grade for the semester was a B. That was the first of many incidents when someone predicted my doom and I made it my life's mission to prove that person wrong. That was also a revelation that with determination and stubbornness, I could accomplish just about anything!

I was now a complete metamorphosis of my former self. Although I was "in this world," I was now following the church's dictates, striving mightily not to be "of this world." That was probably the one guidepost that steered me clear of experimenting with tobacco, alcohol, drugs, and sex. For most of my high school experience I was like an invisible fly on the wall, watching my classmates bumping their heads on life.

❦ MAMA BEGAN TO LOOK OLD ❦

Mrs. Peterson's kids were now grown, but her elderly, ailing mother had moved in. Over the years, Mrs. Peterson had noticed how quickly Mama completed her duties, and she felt that Mama needed something else to fill her day. Mama needed the money, so she figured eight hours was eight hours. The old woman slept most of the day, but the problem came when Mama was required to lift her in order to change the bed. Mama never questioned. She only complied. In the evenings when the city transit buses offloaded dozens of domestic workers, Mama was most identifiable by her bent back and stooped shoulders. The lines on her face traced the weariness in her soul. Mama began to look old.

❦ THE LONG, HOT SUMMER ❦

The only furniture in the second room on the right were beds, at least four of them—no box springs, just a thin mattress atop heavy wire springs. The bunk beds were made of metal. Sometimes they were stacked, sometimes not. To give more floor space, they were placed against the pass-through doors. Beds are used for sleep. Beds are used to rest. Beds can be a source of pleasure. Beds can also be a source of pain.

There will probably be some who think this story should be omitted. Some won't believe the story possible. Still others will suggest quickly that I change the names to avoid embarrassment. I contend that is precisely what perpetrators want, and to do so suggests that the victims should be embarrassed that they were victimized and the perpetrators deserve not to be ashamed.

Mama had made the phone call earlier that Sunday morning. It didn't take long for two of my oldest brothers and their spouses to drop everything and head for our house on Arcadia Circle. Tensions were high, but soon they would become explosive. When I decided to come forward with my information, I thought the only thing that would happen is that one person would be told never to do this thing again, and life would return to normal. However, our reality was anything but normal. If I had any idea that the truth would be twisted around and slapped in our faces, I'm certain I would have kept my mouth shut.

It was a long, hot summer in 1964. The closeness between my sister Lettie and me had begun to wane, partly because of the different friends and activities that we both found once we started high school. We also handled adolescence differently. From an early age Lettie had a high IQ. She was also a tomboy. She had a mental and physical advantage over almost everyone, including the boys. She exerted this advantage at will, which obviously kept her in a lot of trouble; soon anything she said became suspect. I, on the other hand, was skinny, timid, and gullible and wanted to be accepted. Consequently I would do almost anything to get others to be my friend. We both still got into trouble and still played hard but not together. The severity of her antics always outshone mine.

When I say that our family's reality was anything but normal, I am referring to our sleeping arrangements. My sister, a teenage brother, and I occupied the second room on the right. Since we were siblings, my mother never thought this was a cause for concern. Neither did I, until that night. When I say we played hard, I mean *hard*—so much so that when we went to sleep, we were almost comatose. For ten years I was a bed wetter who could sleep soundly in soaked pajamas all night and be utterly surprised (and ashamed) when I woke the next morning. By my teen years I no longer played as hard, didn't sleep as soundly, and my bedwetting days were behind me. At the age of sixteen Lettie still slept so soundly and snored so loudly that sometimes it was almost impossible to wake her. When her body had enough sleep, she woke up easily.

That night, Lettie was sleeping in a single bed that had been placed perpendicular to the bunk bed. The bunk bed was occupied by my older brother and me. As was the custom, the youngest always had the bottom bed.

One night I awakened to find my older brother on top of Lettie. He was so bold that he left on the ceiling light. Even more amazing was I could still hear Lettie snoring as loudly as always. I didn't think he was penetrating her at the time, because honestly I didn't know what penetration was. At the age of fourteen, I still did not understand what was going on with my own changing body, much less that of an adolescent boy. To understand the level of my naiveté or ignorance, I had been menstruating for three years before I found out the source of the blood.

I watched my brother's actions with my sister quietly several times and never said anything to anyone. Then one night it happened. I was awakened by a tug on my pajamas. I was his new victim. When I woke up and grabbed the waistband of my pajamas, he was startled and retreated to his bed. On the next night, my brother began steadily rocking the top bed, perhaps to lull me to sleep. After about thirty minutes I saw him looking down over the side of the bed to see if I was asleep. I no longer trusted my ability to sleep lightly enough to protect myself.

On the next night I got four safety pins and pinned my pajamas to the sheets. On his next visit, he couldn't understand why my pajamas did not easily slide down my bony hips. If he applied more force, he would most certainly awaken me. In the morning, I unpinned myself and immediately told Lettie that I had seen our brother on top of her. With a look of shock on her face she replied, "I kept wondering why I'd wake up with my panties down!" She decided to tell Mama right away. Big mistake. Of course my brother immediately denied it, but the big shocker was Mama. She, having given birth to eleven children herself, said, "First, there is no way she could have slept through something like that. Second, a brother would never do that to his sister. Finally, Lettie is a big liar and troublemaker."

At that very minute, two older brothers burst through the front door. One of them instantly grabbed my brother by his neck and pinned him against the wall and shouted, "Boy, I'll kill you!" It was at that point that I came to know that my older brothers realized, for reasons obvious to them, that ours was not a good sleeping arrangement. Tears and tempers reverberated around the room for what seemed like hours. When it was apparent that Mama would not be convinced of my brother's guilt, my older brother said, "Get him out of that room!" We never shared a bedroom again. Lettie told me later that when Daddy came home, she got a beating. She became more rebellious in the following years.

When I started high school, I realized that one of my classmates from elementary school was never around. When I asked where she was, someone said that she had gotten pregnant by her brother. I thought, *Yuck, how could anyone have sex with their brother?* Then I thought, *Perhaps her sleeping arrangement was just like mine.*

The home economics teacher, Laura Woods, was our high school's version of Emily Post. No doubt every female student prior to 1970 had an interesting story to tell about encounters with her. As you may have guessed, mine was tragic—not tragic in the sense of someone dying, but tragic in that she was my last hope in finding an ally in a teacher. Mama had earned quite a reputation for the way she starched and stretched curtains. Laura Woods and her sister became regular customers, and ultimately a friendship developed. Miss Woods believed that one of the requirements for being a proper young lady was wearing proper foundation garments.

Every young lady who took her class had to wear a girdle. Perish the thought that panties and a slip were the only garments beneath our dresses! Miss Woods knew good and well that no one even made a girdle for skinny people like me, who measured nineteen inches in the hips. Mama knew she couldn't afford one even if they did. Since there was absolutely no exception to Miss Woods's rule, they secretly compromised that I could wear a garter belt instead. I think Miss Woods also promised that she would give me special attention. That was great, but I didn't need it. I had already heard all of the horror stories of what to do and what not to do in her class, and I was prepared. In addition, I had Mama and Miss Woods's friendship on my side, or so I thought.

I was a model student and things were going great. Several weeks into the semester, something happened. For the life of me I can't remember what, but I was accused of something I did not do. I was totally blindsided. My denials were not believed. I had no explanation because I was not even around, involved in, or aware of the incident. The only thing that was acceptable was an apology from me—and that was not about to happen because I had done nothing wrong. Since Miss Woods and Mama were friends, I was sure that Mama could intercede on my behalf and come to some kind of truce, as they had done on the garter belt issue. No such luck. Mama said, "You calling grown folk a liar? Grown folk wouldn't say it if they didn't see you do it!" Perhaps she also thought that I had slipped back into my nasty ways of stubbornness.

When it became obvious that I could not prove my innocence and I would not apologize, I made a request to drop her class. It was granted. For the remaining years at Booker T. Washington, I avoided Miss Woods and never spoke to her again. For the remaining years that we lived in the same neighborhood I refused to even walk on the side of the street where she lived. I no longer had a reason or desire to lie, but no one believed me. I thought, *Maybe telling the truth is not all that it's cracked up to be.*

1965

Life After Death

When I came home from school, the smell of him was still everywhere. Perhaps the stench was stronger in my mind because after several days the smell was not as strong. As I passed the living room I was startled by the sight and sound of a massive creature. He was asleep in the corner chair—actually, more than asleep; he was dead drunk. His head, beaded with sweat, appeared too heavy for his neck to support. His opened mouth spewed snorts, grunts, and irregular gasps for air. A large wet circle spotted the front of his pants.

Daddy was now coming home more often and staying longer each time he came. At first I was sure that his new schedule was all because of me. I avoided him whenever possible, and we rarely exchanged words. The atmosphere was much different than before. In the past he never drank at home because he knew it upset Mama. Now that he was home more often, he drank anyway and slept most of the time, even while Mama nagged. Mama was working two full-time jobs. Daddy seemed to be working less. Something else had changed. By the movement of his chest I knew he was still breathing, but now there seemed to be no life. By the way he beat us I thought he had no heart, but now it seemed as if he had no soul. That big mass of flesh seemed empty as if he had given up all hope, all desire, all trying. Perhaps he no longer cared about living. I didn't care if he lived either.

Mama used to fill a room with her presence just by breathing, but now there seemed to be less of her. She no longer nagged Daddy about not bringing money home. No one talked of his not working. The arguments were now about something else. He seldom moved from his chair. When he did, it was slowly. I didn't know it, but Daddy was seriously ill. Many of the details of his illness escape me. The only thing I knew for sure was that he was too weak to ever beat me again. For that I was thankful.

I overheard snatches of arguments between them concerning some kind of surgery at a place called Emory University Hospital. By this time, Daddy's weight had soared to more than 300 pounds and his drinking had taken its toll. He found it difficult to stand for long hours cooking on the train or really doing anything else. Unable to make a stab at financially supporting his family, he discovered that he could get disability if he could prove he had a debilitating medical condition. He had heard of a new medical procedure to put tubes in the heart. Mama was adamantly against it. Her position was that the surgery was experimental, risky, and cost money we didn't have. Daddy wanted it. His position was that after this surgery was performed, he could get disability income. That way, both could benefit: He would no longer have to work, and she could get the money that she was always nagging him about.

July heat in Atlanta is no joke. That July the temperature soared outside, and the tension inside kept pace. By midsummer Daddy's condition was worse. He was literally gasping for air. When I was fifteen, important family information was still kept from me. I don't know whether it was thought that I was still too immature to process it or whether this was customary for all other families at the time. July 15, 1965, was a normal summer day for me, and I was in the living room admiring the light-skinned black women on the cover of *Ebony* magazine. Little did I know that Daddy's experimental open-heart surgery had been scheduled for the same day. Although finances were still tight, Daddy had recently bought Mama the bedroom set that she had always wanted—the first one she would ever have, perhaps to bribe her to agree with the surgery. The deep cherry wood bedroom suite came with several pieces. It was too much for such a small space, and no one cared that there was hardly enough room to stand. What was important was that she had it. That cramped space became the center of all activities within the next twenty-four hours.

I got the news late that night when my sister Sarah came home, visibly shaken. Next Mama came through the doorway, supported on both sides by my brothers. She was in worse shape. Daddy was dead. Sarah said the surgeon came to the waiting room and announced that the surgery was a success, meaning that they found out everything they needed to know. The doctor's next words stunned them all: "But we lost him."

The next day began Mama's period of mourning. Someone had bought her a fancy white nightgown, and she stayed in bed all day, receiving condolences and well wishes from the neighbors. This was the first time that death had touched me so closely. I didn't know how to respond.

When the major breadwinner in a family dies, it usually means that harder times are not too far behind. At last, we beat the odds. Because Daddy died with four minor children, Mama received monthly checks from the Social Security Administration and his retirement fund. Now we could finally have three meals a day, lunch money, and decent clothes. The utilities were never disconnected again. This money would continue for each of us until we reached the age of twenty-one if we remained in school. Now it was possible for me to go further in school, but still, all I wanted was to get farther away from Arcadia Circle.

The most dramatic and immediate benefit of Daddy's death came only sixty days later. After Mama had settled all of the funeral expenses, she agreed to give me fifty dollars a month to buy my own personal items. My first purchase was eyeglasses.

As the huge orange public transportation bus approached, I could hear the gears shift long before I could read the routing sign above its windshield. This was the second time that I made this trip alone. At the age of fifteen, I was certainly old enough to go downtown unaccompanied, but I was scared. I knew the faces of everyone in my neighborhood, but the faces of the people downtown were blank. The cars in my neighborhood stopped when we ran into the streets, but the cars downtown moved faster than I could run. The rooftops of houses on Arcadia Circle opened up a view of the sky in our neighborhood, but the tall buildings downtown seemed to close up the sky on every corner. I knew how to pronounce and spell every street in my neighborhood without looking at the signs, but I knew that it was useless looking at the street signs downtown. By now I knew how nervous and unsettled I became when I was introduced to a stranger or a new environment. I knew how people hated to repeat themselves after only a simple statement. I knew that I tripped over curbs and could never see how I really looked in a mirror.

Several weeks earlier, on my first solo visit to downtown Atlanta, I left home two hours before my scheduled appointment, more than enough time to manage the unknowns. My heightened anxiety prompted me to get off the bus too soon, causing me to walk three extra blocks to the doctor's office. Pearle Optical Store in downtown Atlanta had advertised an eye exam, frames and lenses, plus tax for a whopping twenty-nine dollars and ninety-nine cents! That amount far exceeded anything we could afford prior to Daddy's death. Now the cost was within reach. When I located the white brick building, I lingered in front of the window display for almost an hour.

My choice had already been made. Several weeks before, inside the office lobby, I followed a doctor in a white physician's lab coat into an adjoining examination room. In that room I had my first eye exam, my first diagnosis, my first pair of corrective lenses, and my first day of sight.

I walked out of Pearle Optical in Five Points. I stood on the corners of Auburn Avenue and Peachtree Streets and marveled at the skyline of downtown Atlanta. I looked up just beyond the tallest building, and I swear I could see all the way to Texas. For the first time in my life I could look across the street and read a street sign. I could see the address on a storefront. I could now see how high to step in order to avoid stumbling on the curb. I could now see facial features on people more than an arm's length away. I could look in the mirror and see how I looked with glasses on. Reading my school textbooks was no longer a struggle. My new eyesight gave me a brand-new life! I now literally read anything and everything that was in my visual path, and I delighted in the feeling that my newfound knowledge gave me. Everything that I learned in school, I wanted to take it to the next level.

No matter how well I performed on testing, no matter how many right answers I got in class, and no matter what grade appeared on my report card, I still felt as if I lacked that special edge to compete. Although field trips were not the norm in high school, whenever awards were given for anything, I was edged out by classmates who had a list of field trips to their credit. I don't know of any real useful information that my classmates obtained from those trips. Perhaps it was the social and cultural awareness, the lack of which perhaps may have affected my thinking and actions in the years that followed.

My improved vision dramatically increased my mobility, but trying to get to the public library and back before dark and certainly before mealtime was still a challenge. It was about that time that a white salesperson came to our house selling the World Book Encyclopedia. I know now that even back then, there were systems in place for salespeople to know when someone came into money. The only times a white person had ever set foot inside that house was when the insurance man came once a month to collect on a five-cent life insurance policy that Mama carried. Regardless of the encyclopedia salesman's motives, his sales pitch worked. I signed up to buy my own personal set of encyclopedias (bookcase and all). My only commitment was seventy-five dollars or the easy payment plan of six dollars a month forever. I chose the forever plan. To this day I don't know how someone was able to enter into a binding contract with a minor. Back in the day, if you did not pay, they actually came back and retrieved the merchandise. That was not about to happen, so I never missed a payment. I finished paying for the World Book purchase by the time I graduated from high school, more than three years later. That bookcase was the first piece of new furniture that ever occupied a space in the second room on the right.

Each night I eagerly feasted on facts, dined on data, and drank the ink from the colorful pages. My Pearle Optical cat's-eye glasses and the World Book were my best friends. I fell asleep many nights with my glasses on my face and an encyclopedia on my chest. Soon the twisted frames sat lopsided on my face. I looked just like a crazy woman, but I didn't care. I was a smart one. Over the next two years I did not stop until I had read each volume cover to cover. It was then that I fell in love with words, their correct pronunciation and their captivating power. I became obsessed with having good penmanship because I didn't want anyone to think I couldn't spell simply because they couldn't read my writing. My grades skyrocketed and on the wings of that rocket sat my self-esteem.

It was a dream but it seemed so real. The left side of my face throbbed with pain, pain that had no origin. The surface felt numb, and I was certain that whatever struck me had left a crease on my face. I turned around and there he was. I recognized the boyish face but the long body that towered over me was strange. The question mark faded from my forehead when my eyes aligned with his. It was James Wilson. He didn't have to say a word. He was bigger. He was back. This was payback. I thought his mama told him he couldn't hit girls? Maybe his daddy told him something different. Maybe his daddy is now hitting his mama. If so, then maybe his mama is now a stupid woman, just like my mama said. I had bullied him eight years earlier. I couldn't believe he remembered, much less wanted to retaliate. I suppose the things that you don't understand are the ones you remember most.

Neither James nor I spoke. Memories and emotions spoke louder. His face was blank of emotions. Now he was tall and kind of cute. His once timid eyes now seemed dreamy. Now I had more than one reason to forgive him, but the words couldn't come out. I tried to speak but couldn't move my lips. Something rough and fleshy was clamping my lips together. I shook my head to loosen its grip, and my eyes opened to see Henry hovering over me, pinching my lips together. He was playing another one of his practical jokes. This was another one of those mornings when I had awakened to find that I had fallen asleep reading the encyclopedia. The long crease down the side of my face aligned perfectly with the hard edges of the green and white encyclopedia. I had fallen asleep reading Volume H, about horses: "A horse with a broken leg is unable to stand . . . and will develop nasty sores and can be expected to die a slow and painful death." That bit of information didn't have any significance at the time.

1966

Temperance

Tent revivals, youth federations, and camp meetings were annual, highly anticipated events for Adventists in the 1960s. In the South, the Adventist campground in Florida was the destination for most family vacations. Most of us slept in tents, battled mosquitoes, and shared communal showers and toilets. The upper echelon had cinder-block cabins that had no plumbing but did offer relief from insects. All of us shared communal meals in a dining hall. The weeklong event offered crafts for children, fun and games for teens, and a different speaker each night for the adults. The highlight and culmination of the event was the heralded Youth Temperance Oratorical Contest. America's teens were on the cusp of experimenting with sex, drugs, and alcohol. Perhaps this was the church's way of getting teens to talk to other teens and talk each other out of developing bad habits.

My successful performance in the seventh-grade school play had given me confidence to enter the contest. I chose the topic "Alcoholism." My World Book Encyclopedias didn't have much information on addiction, but my experience living with an alcoholic father had given me all the script I needed. I had seen former contestants fail miserably and others take the plunge and the prize. My stubbornness gave me the determination to snatch the win, and I did. I brought the audience members to their feet with my closing remark: "Wine is a marker; strong drink is raging." The first-place prize was a small scholarship, redeemable only at an Adventist college. Now I had one less excuse for not going to college and one more incentive to take the next step.

❧ TEMPTATION ❧

I was sixteen when I had my first boyfriend. It went without saying that he was also an Adventist because our religion stressed the biblical admonition to "be ye not unequally yoked." The church elders interpreted this scripture to mean, first and foremost, that both partners had to be of the same religion. It didn't matter whether you had compatible personalities, likes, desires, or goals. You pretty much got a boyfriend or girlfriend whenever, if ever, someone looked as if they weren't doing anything else.

Like most girls in high school, I often fantasized about having a boyfriend. If a boy just glanced at us twice or ever made eye contact, that was our clue that he liked us. Never mind that he may have been cross-eyed or worse yet just as confused as we were. The scribbling on our canvas notebooks told the world who loves whom. Imaginary boyfriends made us feel special. A real boyfriend was rare.

My first boyfriend was two years older and dark-skinned like me. He was slim, but he lifted weights. His tight muscles and biceps were easily visible beneath his shirts. He had finely chiseled features and an easygoing personality. He was also an orphan who had witnessed his father murder his mother. His family was fragmented, and his siblings were scattered. He felt alienated and alone; I felt the same but for different reasons. Aside from skin color and religion, alienation and loneliness were our only common ground. He wanted to find a home. I was looking to get away from mine. We both thought we could fulfill the other's needs, so we planned to get married as soon as I finished high school.

The Vietnam War was now in full bloom, and the Selective Service was in high gear. This war saw the highest proportion of blacks ever to serve in an American war. During the height of the U.S. involvement, 1965–69, blacks made up 12.6 percent of the soldiers in Vietnam. The percentage of black combat fatalities in that period was a staggering 14.9 percent. Volunteers and draftees included many frustrated blacks who were impatient with the war and the delays in racial progress in America, which led to race riots. Young black men who had aspirations to further their education scrambled to find ways to dodge or at least delay the draft. My boyfriend did not have the armor of "educational aspirations." His only shield was his religious belief of nonviolence. Before I could finish high school he was drafted into the military as a conscientious objector. The price of stamps was five cents, and I wrote him love letters every day. I decided to go to college only to bide my time until he returned and because I knew that going to college would please Mama.

In the fall of that year, my sister Lettie went away to college. I was now the oldest living at home. The house was less crowded, and the second room on the right now belonged only to me. I got rid of the extra beds and kept two, one to go on each side of my rack of encyclopedias. The bed I slept in was next to the window. The other bed, used for storage, was placed against the attic door. A small gas space heater was on the adjacent wall.

The upper blade of the ceiling fans lazily twirled to the left, the middle blade twirled to the right, and the lower one spun so fast it created a gray haze. All three worked in unison above white-globed lights that hung from the high ceiling of the Ashby Five & Dime Store. This store was one of the only three white-owned establishments in our neighborhood. This store was also the only one whose name boasted the price of its merchandise, yet I could never find anything there that my nickel could buy. That didn't keep me from trying.

The high gloss on the plank floors dulled beneath random layers of dust. The air had a delightful smell that was unique to this store. I thought that was how white people smelled, and I liked it. I later learned that the smell was mothballs. Blacks were not permitted to enter unless there was at least one white person to guard each black person. The lights were bright even in the daytime. This enabled the merchants to see what they thought was certain to happen whenever a colored person entered the store. The store's merchandise was displayed on large wooden tables that stood waist-high to an adult. When Henry and I were younger, we stood just tall enough for those table heights to dissect our bodies just above our shoulders. When the store owners saw two round nappy heads bobbing down the aisles, they immediately jumped to their feet and followed our every move. I thought this was attentive, personalized service. Henry knew differently and decided to have some fun. Every so often Henry would reach for an item on the table then quickly hide his hand behind his back. The white merchant sprang into action, twisting Henry's arm and prying his hands open, only to find nothing. Henry's big, wide grin cut like a knife. The merchant's disappointment paled in comparison to his embarrassment.

I decorated my room with lavender curtains from that store. Neither of my two bedspreads matched. The lavender in my new curtains matched nothing in the room either. I didn't care. I kept my room clean and orderly. At last I had my own private space. I forbade anyone to enter without my permission. Absolutely no one could touch my encyclopedias without my consent.

Not As Things First Appear

Inside of my clean and cozy room, my new set of encyclopedias was a startling contrast to the oldness of everything else. The twenty-two volumes stood at attention in the pine bookcase. The white Naugahyde cover of each book was the background for a gold world globe and gold and green letters. The spine of each book had an olive green panel that was the background for more gold lettering that referenced the specific volume. That bookcase and its contents were the only thing right about that room. Every couple of weeks I rearranged the beds just to give it a fresh new look. I could tell instantly if anyone had touched anything. My newfound sight gave me the confidence to venture farther away from home. A few dollars in my pocket and public transportation gave me the means to do it more often. Countless nights of falling asleep in my eyeglasses now left them so twisted that they slid easily off my face. The optician had agreed to adjust them, but I had to get to his office by five o'clock. I decided to go immediately after school was dismissed at three-thirty.

That January school day began as a cold and frigid one. By noon the sun had warmed the air to just above freezing, but afternoon arctic winds had caused the thermometer to return to the predawn temperature. My bus rides had become frequent, and I took a window seat just behind the driver. The bus route was a straight shot down Hunter Street into downtown Atlanta. Each trip gave me the opportunity to fixate on details that I had never noticed before.

At the Chestnut Street stop I studied the discolored bricks in West Hunter Street Baptist Church. As we approached the Vine Street stop, near the Morris Brown clock tower, this was the first time that I could read the Roman numerals on the huge time machine. The Phillis Wheatley YWCA was the last brick structure that filled my windowpane before I saw a long row of weathered clapboard apartments on the left just beyond Maple Street. Patches of brown winter grass dotted a muddy yard. Rusted engines, hollowed car bodies, and an oil drum sat in shallow cradles. The two-story dwellings staggered like drunkards on top of shifting foundations, amid garbage and debris. Beer bottles, water-stained cardboard boxes, and trash littered the stairs. A metal bucket full of rainwater with a thick layer of ice on top sat in the alley. Many of the windows were covered with plastic or cardboard, all of them in need of repair.

The only signs of life were a small listless child and a stray pregnant dog, nosing the ground for food. At first glance, the girl appeared frozen in time, stuck in deprived surroundings. Her only protection from the frigid weather was a cotton headscarf and a sweater with two missing buttons. Her spindly legs were ashy, and her knocked knees trembled fiercely. She was so congested with mucus that her breathing appeared labored.

My heart was quickened by her and strangely drawn to her at the same time. Moments earlier I had looked out of that window and seen a little girl. Now that same window was a mirror and I saw me. There were many wintry days that I walked to school with no boots, gloves, or overcoat. My long, skinny frame resulted in my hand-me-down clothes never fitting properly. We never had toboggans or hats, only plastic rain bonnets, even when it was not raining. Mama believed that the plastic made our head sweat and more warmth was generated that way than with a thin cotton scarf. I never stayed home with a cold. Instead I coughed, sneezed, and blew my nose around anyone and everyone. My lips were often chapped, so I licked them constantly for relief. A painful scabby sore encircled my mouth, and I soon bore a strong resemblance to a raccoon. I also remembered being plagued with a skin disease called tetter, which made my short, thin hair even more unmanageable. In warmer weather I suffered with outbreaks of ringworm on my face and arms. Perhaps my classmates avoided me because I looked strange. Perhaps they viewed me with the same set of eyes that I now saw this little girl. Perhaps they avoided me and perceived me as one big germ.

The neighbors rarely and my teachers certainly never saw Daddy because of his long hours on the railroad. Whenever they saw Mama, she was usually pregnant. Her two full-time jobs prevented her from attending any school functions. Perhaps the teachers' mindless teasing was generated by the false assumption that Mama never legally married and bore eleven children out of wedlock. That was the first day that I realized that maybe some things are not always as they first appear.

When I returned from downtown I rushed to the comfort of my bedroom. The small gas heater kept the room's temperature warmer than any other place in the house. Upon entering my room I sensed that something had changed. Anything so slight was major. I felt it in my gut before I saw it with my eyes. The beds were untouched. The window was in the same position. The clothes still hung behind the door, and the pilot light flickered in the small heater. When I looked at my set of World Book Encyclopedias I noticed that they were not in order. Someone had used one and had placed it back in the rack upside down. I was furious! It had to be Henry. Who else would dare to come into my room?

Because of his physical strength I knew better than to approach him on my own, so I went to the kitchen to tell Mama. At the same time Henry was coming through the back door. I screamed, "Mama, Henry has been in my room and was messing with my encyclopedias!" Henry's reply was, "Girl, I don't care nothin' about dem psycho-pedias." By this time I had already positioned myself safely behind Mama when I swung at him and I said, "Yes, you did!" When Henry swung back, Mama blocked his blow. I'm glad she did. She stopped the fight before I got hurt. I went back to my room to look for any other damage to my books. I found out later that it wasn't Henry who had taken an interest in the World Book series. It was Mama.

I don't know exactly when Mama stopped working as a domestic for Mrs. Peterson. With Daddy's monthly Social Security check, her nighttime job cleaning the bank, and fewer of us still at home, there certainly was no need to.

That year we got our first new sofa. It was an Early American style with tufted arms and a winged back. The black-and-white print not only dominated the small living room, but this lone piece of furniture stuck out like a sore thumb, especially against the backdrop of the sky-blue hand-me-down curtains. The other brand-new addition to the living room was a large rectangular picture of the Lord's Last Supper. Mama proudly hung it on the wall above the gas heater. Sometime later I came home to find a gold metal frame hanging on the adjoining wall. The eight-foot wall immediately appeared much larger, only because of the small object hanging on its surface. On closer inspection I saw that Mama had happened upon a poem by Rudyard Kipling. The poem had been cut from the pages of a magazine and had been placed neatly between the frame's cardboard backing and the thin layer of glass. The poem was Rudyard Kipling's "If":

IF
If you can keep your head when all about you
are losing theirs and blaming it on you;
If you can trust yourself when all men doubt you,
but make allowance for their doubting too:
If you can wait and not be tired by waiting,
or, being lied about, don't deal in lies,
Or being hated don't give way to hating,
and yet don't look too good, nor talk too wise;
If you can dream—and not make dreams your master;
if you can think—and not make thoughts your aim,
if you can meet with Triumph and Disaster
and treat those two impostors just the same:
If you can bear to hear the truth you've spoken
twisted by knaves to make a trap for fools,
or watch the things you gave your life to, broken,
and stoop and build 'em up with worn-out tools;
If you can make one heap of all your winnings

and risk it on one turn of pitch-and-toss,
and lose, and start again at your beginnings,
and never breathe a word about your loss:
If you can force your heart and nerve and sinew
to serve you turn long after they are gone,
and so hold on when there is nothing in you
except the Will which says to them: "Hold on!"
If you can talk with crowds and keep your virtue,
or walk with Kings—nor lose the common touch,
if neither foes nor loving friends can hurt you,
if all men count with you, but none too much:
If you can fill the unforgiving minute
with sixty seconds' worth of distance run,
Yours is the Earth and everything that's in it,
and—which is more—you'll be a Man, my son!

I then realized that the Bible wasn't Mama's only source of strength. The newspaper headline was not the only print she pondered. Thinking back over the years I remember how she began consulting us for the correct pronunciation of any word she did not know. As Mama was being pushed through life, she was picking up knowledge along the way. She picked up social graces by working as a domestic. She gained knowledge of world affairs by likening every world or national event as an Armageddon to the Lord's return. She knew how to run a household on ten cents or less. Amid all the chaos in her life, she listened; she studied people's actions and reactions. She learned that common sense was not common to everyone. She respected authority, and she knew how to use hers. She learned that you couldn't always wait for your ship to come in; sometimes you have to swim out to get it. She learned some hard lessons from the school of hard knocks. I learned that she was a force to be reckoned with. Although she only had a tenth-grade education, Mama was no doubt the smartest person in that house.

By now it was obvious to all that Henry had developed a fascination with cars. The '57 Chevy caught his eye. He studied everything about it—inside and out. His dream car had a white top, the lower body sported a candy-apple red color, and it had whitewall tires to match. Its form was bold but not bulky. It was a well-oiled and fine-tuned machine. It had power. It had speed. It was somewhere between sporty and classy. It personified everything that he was not, yet everything that he could become. Henry spent countless days and hours in solitude studying the intricate parts of this machinery. In the absence of criticism, he made mistakes and figured out the solution. Whatever he damaged, he learned how to repair it. He soon learned how interdependent each part was, and he could quickly and correctly diagnose any malfunction. Within his own rights and in the minds of those who knew him, he became more than just an auto mechanic. He became a skilled mechanical engineer. With no funds to finance his passion, Henry soon found that he could steal parts cheaper and quicker than he could purchase them. Mind you, he had no qualms about paying for the premium oils and lubricants. He could not chance inferior products harming his prized possession.

Henry left home every morning as if he were going to school, but his grades indicated that his mind went somewhere else. He chose to take Russian as his foreign language elective. He got an A in Russian but he got an F in physical education. While the others were excelling, Henry was failing. All of Henry's infractions with the law were auto-related, and they ranged in severity from a misdemeanor to aggravated assault on a police officer. Within a relatively short period of time, he became skillful enough to steal a car and have it completely disassembled in two hours before the owner could report it missing. With very little effort (some say with his eyes closed and single-handedly) he could build a car from the stolen parts within one week. Henry was unequivocally guilty in every case, but he showed absolutely no remorse. He never offered an apology, rationale, or excuse for his behavior. Decades later he stated boldly, "I am a professional criminal, and this is what professionals do."

Mama now began the practice of using hard-earned money to bail him out of jail. Mama felt the only excuse she needed was that he was her child.

1968

For a Heavenly Cause

My senior class activities had begun, and my investiture ceremony three days earlier validated that I had completed all requirements to receive my high school diploma. With graduation less than two months away, I settled in front of the television to catch the late-night news. The television screen flashed scenes of a motel, then a hospital, crowds gathering, people crying, police, and news media. It took me a few seconds to realize what had happened. I was so busy preparing for my upcoming graduation that I didn't realize that Martin Luther King was scheduled to march in Memphis. The broadcast was already in progress. The screen flashed,

DR. MARTIN LUTHER KING JR.
HAS BEEN ASSASSINATED

By now, the news had reached the far corners of the globe, and heads of states, prime ministers, and dignitaries were commenting on the nation's tragedy. The television flashed scenes of rioting, looting, and burnings. Suddenly I was struck with fear. I thought the world was ending. Was this the Armageddon that the Adventists had preached about?

King was pronounced dead at St. Joseph Hospital at 7:05 p.m. on April 4, 1968. Within hours, the poor colored sections of more than 100 cities went up in flames.

The next scene on the television screen was of President Lyndon Johnson expressing sadness and pleading for the nation's calm. As I began to grasp the full impact of what had happened, the sun began to set and a dark cloud covered the sky. As I sat motionless, digesting the details, a bolt of lightning lit up the night and a deafening thunder shattered the silence. The thick, dark cloud that had ushered the setting sun now opened the floodgates and loosed its torrential waters. It was a rainy night in Georgia. I had never seen it rain like that before. It was as if all of heaven and earth were crying.

Every television station had preempted all programming to cover the assassination, the aftermath, and the funeral.

On April 9, 1968, a procession of more than 200,000 mourners—famous and unknown, rich and poor, powerful and weak—poured into Atlanta by the thousands and by any means necessary to follow King's coffin being pulled through the streets of Atlanta.

Two and a half decades later the world came to town again but for a happier event.

❀ FOR A HEAVENLY CAUSE ❀

On that spring day in May there was not a cloud in the sky, but I was on cloud nine. I had already ordered my cap and gown, taken senior pictures, got autographs in my yearbook, and sent out invitations. In less than four weeks I was scheduled to be in my first march, the graduation march to receive my high school diploma. This was the decade of the golden oldies. The music was golden—"Let's Twist Again" by Chubby Checker, and "Walk on By" by Dionne Warwick. Television sitcoms were golden—The Jackie Gleason Show and The Andy Griffith Show.

In the late '60s, a high school diploma was a great accomplishment; for me, it was better than gold. This was my biggest accomplishment, at least one that came with recognition. This was my opportunity to get something my parents never had; it was a relief that I had made it. Graduating made me believe that I could go further. I hurried home from school, gingerly clutching the box that held my graduation cap and gown.

Man of La Mancha was playing on Broadway, and its well-known song "The Impossible Dream" had been chosen as our class song. I learned it quickly, for it seemed that every word of the lyrics spoke to me. My head was bigger than the room, and it was in my head that these words and my interpretation of them resounded. Prancing around the room I sang,

> To dream the impossible dream, to fight the unbeatable foe.
> *(Miss Carter was a foe who said I'd never pass her class. I
> proved her wrong. I had been an honor roll student since
> sophomore year.)*
> To bear with unbearable sorrow, to run where the brave dare not go.
> *(Some classmates dropped out, some got pregnant, several went
> to jail, two were killed, but I stayed focused; I made it.)*
> To right the unrightable wrong, to love, pure and chaste from afar.
> *(I never went to a prom, or attended a football game. But I'm
> going to my graduation.)*
> To try, when your arms are too weary, to reach the unreachable star.
> *(Academically I ranked number thirty-one in a class of more
> than 600 seniors. Not bad for someone who had just awakened
> from near blindness only three years earlier.)*

I strutted like a peacock, catching a glimpse of my image in the dusty windowpane ahead. Turning away I looked over my right shoulder and tossed my tassel with the same flair that the longhaired girls toss their ponytails! I counted the days. I rehearsed my smile. I practiced saying, "Thank you." I couldn't wait for that big night.

Booker T. Washington High School had a proud history of orchestrating one of the most dramatic commencement ceremonies in the Atlanta Auditorium. People came from miles around just to see the unique production. Each graduate was positioned in the procession line so that when seated, the girls' white attire formed the background and the boys' black attire formed the graduation year. Preparation for graduation took weeks of planning and coordination from the administration. Years of experience meant the process was now down to a fine science. Everyone involved had to be in place and on time. The date was set for May 25, 1968.

As a practicing Seventh Day Adventist, observing Saturday as the true biblical day of worship (Sabbath), all members were admonished to abstain from all secular activities from sunset Friday until sunset Saturday. True observance also meant guarding the edges of the Sabbath—no fudging of minutes. This ritual was adhered to so strictly that the next week's exact time of sunset was printed in the previous week's church bulletin (probably from the *Farmer's Almanac*).

Our commencement was scheduled for Saturday, eight o'clock in the evening. The Sabbath would be over at seven o'clock. No fudging, no problem—I could participate. Ten days before the event, the most important and final rehearsal was set for seven o'clock on Friday evening—the beginning of the Sabbath. If I didn't attend this rehearsal I would not be allowed to participate in the graduation. Back in my bedroom that night, calm had changed to calamity as I struggled to find a solution.

The next morning I timidly approached my homeroom teacher and explained the Adventist doctrine and asked for an exception. His response was, "No. Everyone has to be at all rehearsals or you will not march." I was so self-conscious and timid that I cried easily when I was denied even the simplest request. The stars in my eyes dissolved into tears as I pondered how quickly everything was falling apart.

Next I sought the help of my church. Surely they could explain my dilemma better than I. Surely they had a workable solution. I don't know if the minister ever tried to intercede. What I do know for sure is that I never received a return call and the decision was not reversed. Mama was aware of my quandary, but remember, she admired teachers so much she truly believed they were next to God and could do no wrong. She never questioned any church directive. Furthermore, if the pastor could not fix the problem, what power did she have?

Many alternatives ran through my mind. The best ones I put to the test. Choice by meticulous choice, I swam through the sludge. I knew what I had to do. I made an appointment to speak with Mr. Moreland, the school's principal.

❦ A MATTER OF PRINCIPLE ❦

At 3:30 in the afternoon, the halls at school were nearly empty—just traces of students and teachers dotted the campus. Shortly after the dismissal bell rang, I found myself seated on a hard wooden bench in the waiting area in the main office. Although I had requested a meeting with the head principal, I got his assistant, Mr. Jackson, instead. I guess Mr. Moreland's time was reserved for the more serious matters, such as someone being stabbed or being caught destroying school property or, at the very least, someone being caught smoking cigarettes.

In years past my trips to the principal's office were not by choice. This office visit would be a defining moment. Within minutes the secretary indicated that Mr. Jackson was ready to see me.

Mr. Jackson's office was easily half the size of our shotgun house on Arcadia Circle. He was seated behind a massive wooden desk. Behind the desk a large window filled the wall from ceiling to floor. The loud roar of the window air conditioner helped to quiet the sound of my racing heart. The cold air blowing through the vents did little for my sweaty palms. Waving a pointed finger, Mr. Jackson motioned me in and ordered me to sit where his finger directed.

Alvin Jackson was in his fifties, slim of build, with wide shoulders and a receding hairline. Peering over his black bifocals, he met my eyes. Mine twitched. Sitting relieved the pressure from my rubbery kneecaps. While shuffling papers on his desk and barking orders to someone on the other end of his phone, his glance made it clear that I was a distraction. After what seemed like forever, he leaned back in this chair and asked the purpose of this meeting. Trying to prepare the platform for my request, my voice cracked as I slowly stated my name, classification, and grade point average. At this point Mr. Jackson leaned forward, and his body language told me to get to the point and stop wasting his time. Quickly and nervously I tried to explain Adventism. All attempts to get special permission to attend all practices except on Friday night were met with the answer no. I asked if someone could stand in for me and then I could take my rightful seat on graduation night. The same answer was no. I asked if they could start the rehearsal one hour earlier so that I could be finished before the Sabbath arrived. The answer was unequivocally *no*.

I received no help from any civil libertarians, no help from the school board, no media attention, no help from the church, and no help from Mama. I pleaded to everyone who had any power, including God. Surely fasting, praying, and reading my Bible would turn things around at the last minute. I was stupid with stubbornness—the same stubbornness that Daddy tried to beat out of me. Mama thought that teachers were God-sent. I felt that neither God nor the teachers were on my side. It was me against the world.

My gown was now pressed and hanging on the hook on the attic door. It was graduation night, and the Sabbath was over. The sun had set and slivers of light from the hallway filtered beneath my door. A breeze from the open window swirled the hem of the white graduation gown, and it danced like a ghost. My pain was so strong that I didn't realize that my darkest moment was a positive, life-changing event.

Still, I imagined myself already in the lineup, preparing to make my grand entrance. As more than 600 classmates marched into the Atlanta Auditorium without question or pause, I cried in the second room on the right and marched into hell for a heavenly cause.

❦ MOVING ON ❦

On the following Monday morning my classmates were still buzzing about the graduation and the after-parties while I tasted the excitement secondhand.

It was now the first of June, and I still had not made application to a college. Over the past few months I had been so consumed with fighting to participate in my graduation that I concentrated on little else. Oakwood College is an Adventist school in Huntsville, Alabama. Everyone naturally assumed that I would go there because of its proximity to Atlanta. Now I was tired and weary of the South. I wanted to get as far away as I could from Atlanta, my high school, the house on Arcadia Circle, and Mama. These were my only criteria for choosing where to attend.

Academically I ranked highly in my class and my GPA was pretty good, so I can't explain why I was so shocked when I received an acceptance letter from Union College in Lincoln, Nebraska. Union College was a small, racially mixed Adventist college. For months Mama and everyone else tried to discourage me from going so far away. Stubborn me said, "I'll go where I want or I won't go at all!"

I remembered how thoroughly Mama had packed for our trip to New York, and I did the same. Since I would be gone for a longer period of time, I packed everything I had. The only thing of value that I owned was my set of encyclopedias, and I knew I could not leave them behind. I spent several hours repacking the twenty-six volumes and the two unabridged dictionaries (and the wooden bookcase). Three days before my flight I paid a taxi to take them to the Greyhound bus depot. My precious cargo would be awaiting my arrival in Nebraska.

On that Thursday night in August when the United Airlines jet pushed away from the gate, I questioned my decision, *What have I done?* My sister Janie had given me my first set of Samsonite luggage. I was now taking my first airplane flight. This would be my first visit to a midwestern state. This was the first time living up close and personal with white people. My stubbornness had backed me into a corner with no way out. I had no knowledge, no experience, no frame of reference, and no concept of how to handle the consequences of what lay ahead. Mama said, "Being grown is more than saying it." My first experience living away from home proved she was right.

My first year at this Adventist college was indeed an eye-opener. This was the first time that I saw how Caucasians' hair became straight when it got wet. I saw how their skin burned and turned red from just a slight exposure to sun. I began to love my black skin. For religious reasons blacks were merely tolerated, not accepted. For religious reasons, all students were required to attend convocation and attend church on the Sabbath, but the black students were allowed to worship at a black church in the community.

Several other memorable things happened during my stay at that school. The monthly check from Daddy's Social Security proved barely enough to cover tuition, books, room, and board. Prior to my leaving home, this would have been Mama's problem. Now it was mine. Was this one of those grown-up things Mama talked about? I found myself penniless within no time. I had to find a job that would pay me cash on the spot.

This was the first time I ever worked as a domestic in a white person's home. Local residents in the surrounding community often advertised for female students to earn extra cash in exchange for light housekeeping. I answered an ad. I arrived at the home of a white lady who would be hosting an elaborate dinner party later that evening. She was going out to shop, and she needed me to clean the living room, dining room, and kitchen before her return. My pay would be eight dollars, and I accepted the job. Her last instruction before she left was, "Oh, and by the way, I need you also to clean the oven."

I took an assessment of the duties and decided to clean the oven first because it was in worse shape, but it was worse than I thought. There was so much grease and baked-on grime that I literally had to chisel my way through the job. When the owner returned three hours later, the house had not been cleaned because I was still on my knees cleaning her oven. She was furious. I explained that cleaning the oven took more time than I anticipated. It was then that she said, "What do you think that can of Easy-Off is for?" I had never heard of Easy-Off. I don't think Mama had either. The woman immediately took me back to campus, ordered me out of her car, and drove off without paying. That was my first and last domestic job.

This was also the first time I ever saw black people who were blacker than I but who didn't consider themselves black. There were only a handful of black students on campus. Several came from Omaha or Kansas, and some came from the islands. I thought it interesting that the students who came from

Trinidad did not associate with the other black students and did not want to be categorized as black.

In the late 1960s the fashion trend had not yet transcended to ladies wearing pantsuits and denim jeans. A girls' dress length was still expected to be comfortably below her knees. Despite the subzero temperature that lingered for much of the school year, the school's handbook specifically prohibited female students from wearing slacks.

The first snowfall came in mid-October. Since the temperature stayed around thirty degrees, the snow decided to stay around also. Snowplows were a stationary fixture on every street. By January, mounds of once-white snow had changed from depressingly dirty to dusty brown and then to gross green.

The frigid temperature was the perfect catalyst for constant colds in my frail frame. A white classmate by the name of Judy easily and often was granted permission to delay assignments and retake tests when she had the slightest discomfort or illness. All of my requests were denied. My grades suffered, and I struggled. I was sick and homesick much of the two years that I attended Union College.

My first Christmas away from home found me in forty-five-degree-below-zero weather, with four feet of snow and all public transportation grounded. I was stranded in Lincoln, Nebraska, suffering with the Hong Kong flu. I hated the day that I became grown!

1969

A Mess in the Midwest

During my second year, the Charles Manson/Sharon Tate massacre occurred. I had read about the Holocaust, but that seemed so far away from my world—almost unbelieveable. But the media kept the Manson/Tate saga in our faces daily and kept me frightened. I don't know what the white Adventists thought, but the black Adventists viewed this as another sign of the Lord's soon return.

Our school's annual picnic was the introduction of spring, much like spring break is for today's college students. I'll never forget the school picnic that was scheduled for May 10, 1969. I anxiously awaited that day, for I needed it to thaw my body and my mind. We woke early that morning only to find that fourteen inches of fresh snow had fallen the night before. The picnic was held in the school cafeteria. I knew then that I could not endure three more years of this. I decided to stay one more year.

During the summer break, the school provided free storage units for returning students to use. Of course this was at our own risk, but I was thankful because it just wasn't practical to take my encyclopedias home for three months. When I returned the next year I never took them out of storage because the library's volumes were more up to date. My two dictionaries were always close by, for a ready reference.

By the end of my second year I was so ready to go home that I left on the day of my last exam. I had just enough money to buy a one-way ticket on Braniff

Airlines. At the time, there was no direct flight from Lincoln to Atlanta. The cheapest ticket had a two-hour layover in Chicago O'Hare International, the world's busiest airport. I didn't even have enough money to buy food, so I went directly to the assigned gate. It was almost two hours prior to scheduled departure and no one else was at the gate, so I decided to take a nap. Two hours later I awoke to find that I was still all alone and the lights appeared to be dimmer. The marquee above the counter displayed a departure time that had expired. I was mildly concerned but nowhere close to the panic that would grip me within the next thirty minutes.

I could not imagine what the problem was, so I asked the first person whom I saw. The only people still milling around in the adjoining gates were the cleaning crew. They knew nothing and advised me to return to the terminal and get information from the reservation desk. I couldn't remember what gate and concourse I was on, but it must have been the one farthest away from my destination. After what seemed like forever I reached the terminal, only to find other passengers in waiting lines two people deep. When I was finally face to face with an airline agent, I was told that my flight had changed gates. I had slept soundly through the announcement. Rescheduling to another flight required a twenty-five-dollar change fee, which I did not have. I had no credit card, and debit cards were unheard of at the time.

When it became apparent to the reservation agent that I was not able to change my flight plans, she asked me to step aside so that she could assist the next passenger. My panic now kicked into high gear. I turned around and faced a sea of strangers. A few of them black; more were obviously foreigners, but most were white. My eyes began to tear, and my bladder began to burn. In the midst of an impending crisis, the strangest thought came across my mind. I thought that perhaps my tear ducts were connected to my urinary tract because one always seemed to trigger the other. When I exited the ladies room my mind was now clear to face the fact that I was now alone 300 miles away from a school that I never wanted to see again and stranded 700 miles away from a home that I'd now give anything to see.

My remaining coins were just enough to make a collect phone call to Mama to ask her to wire funds so that I could get home. I had never wired funds before and knew nothing about it. I'd figure that part out when I got to it. The telephone operator's first attempt to connect me to someone on the other end was met with an unanswered call. Answering machines weren't popular yet, and there was no caller ID to signal that I had called. When I returned the payphone's receiver to the hook, my dime was returned in the slot below and I returned to the scariness of my predicament.

A large wall clock ticked toward 8:20 p.m. Repeated attempts every thirty minutes resulted in more unanswered calls. As long as I could remember, someone had always been in that house. Where was everyone? My panic now escalated. My remaining coins were the only allies that kept me falsely connected to a failing hope on the other end of an unanswered phone. That one remaining friend failed me when the malfunctioning phone failed to return my coins, adding insult to injury. I felt as if I had been robbed. By now I had been in the airport close to six hours and hunger pains began to knot in my stomach. I couldn't risk that hungry payphone eating my last coin. The departure screen on the wall signaled the last flight to Atlanta. Panic now engulfed me, but I dealt with that when I got back from the bathroom.

I suppose this is the point in life when desperate people are forced to dance with the thought of doing desperate things such as stealing, dealing, prostituting, or even harming another, but none of those were a part of my world, so they never entered my thought process. Ironically, that left me with no options, which made my predicament more troubling.

O'Hare International never sleeps, and at any given hour there are always thousands of people at some stage of travel, but I still felt alone. I wandered aimlessly through the crowd, more to flee fear than to seek a solution. In retrospect, I marvel at the next action that I took. This act was not thought out, rehearsed, or even targeted to any specific person. And I definitely had no idea as to how it would turn out. Looking back, it was probably more of my sheer stubbornness not to fail. I timidly approached a white businessman and told him of my plight and asked to borrow twenty-five dollars. Without question or hesitation he pulled the money out of his wallet, placed it in my hand, and walked away. I'm sure I said, "Thank you," but those words bounced off the back of his suit as he disappeared down the concourse. Shock and relief left me momentarily motionless. A blaring loudspeaker announcing the next departing flight brought me back to life. With only pennies and minutes to spare, I was the last passenger to board the last flight to Atlanta. In a matter of hours, I felt that I had aged 100 years. As the huge United jet sped down the runway, a part of me was left in the O'Hare terminal. Once again tears filled my eyes but I held my bladder at bay. The aircraft had just ascended the clouds over Chicago when I realized that I had not made provisions for my encyclopedias to be shipped back to Atlanta. I never saw my encyclopedias again. I also realized that I never got my benefactor's name or an address to return the money.

1970-1972

Carbon Paper and the Original

The reason I could get no one on the phone when I called from the airport was that Mama had been involved in an auto accident. The taxicab in which she was riding had a head-on collision with another vehicle. Mama had sustained head trauma from the impact with the car's windshield. Those were the days before people used seatbelts as much as they do now. Several days of hospitalized observation revealed no permanent or life-threatening injury—or so we thought.

Our family had also moved in the early 1970s away from 97 Arcadia Circle, and Mama finally got her chance to live in a brick house in the Venetian Hills section of town. A brick house in any condition was a coveted possession for most blacks in the South.

Within months my boyfriend returned from Vietnam. To my dismay and surprise, we both had changed. I had gotten a taste of life beyond Atlanta: Now I realized that it was possible to have a better life and maybe education was the way to have it. Many things had changed drastically since King's assassination, but my boyfriend came back to the familiar soil that held memories of his mother's shed blood; on top of that, he had nightmares of the bloodshed on foreign soil.

At long last when we sat side by side on a park bench in Maddox Park, we knew we were still miles apart. The fire, passion, and even the sparks were gone.

We both knew that marriage was not the thing to do. We had to move on. Unable to adjust to the new world around him, he grabbed the reenlistment bonus and returned to the military. With two years of college to my credit, frostbitten feet, a broken heart, and a hesitant head, I decided to finish what I had started—the pursuit of my degree. I enrolled in Clark College.

❧ WHITE FLIGHT, TALK RIGHT ❧

In the early 1970s white flight became widespread and decent housing became affordable for blacks. We moved away from Arcadia Circle to the southwest side of town. This cinder-block bungalow was painted a bright yellow and contained three bedrooms and one bath. Although not much larger than the house we had left, it did have heat in every room, a larger eat-in kitchen, a paved driveway, and a big backyard with fruit trees. The house was much less crowded, and Henry was eager to explore every room and claim a space that was uniquely his. Unlike Arcadia Circle, this house had an attic with pull-down stairs.

One day when Mama was away, Henry tugged on the heavy cord that dangled from the hallway ceiling. The wooden door dropped and stopped in mid-air. On the upper side of the door was a ladder that, when extended, reached to the floor. Henry quickly climbed the stairs with the anticipated excitement of, at the very least, being high enough to look down on me. I told him that I would stay below and alert him if Mama came home early. The real reason was that I was scared. Just beyond the opening to his left was a light fixture with no bulb. Only filtered light from below and the tiny stream of sunlight that sneaked through an air vent ahead split the darkness. His eyes followed the glimmer of light, which provided just enough illumination to reveal a lot of junk that the previous owner had left behind.

Surveying the remaining area required that he adjust himself slightly on the stairs. When he aligned his head with his body, a spider web enveloped his face. He swiped away at the annoying mesh and climbed onto the plywood flooring. The air was thick with the smell of mothballs. It was also musty from dampness and dust, and he quickly sensed the difference in temperature. From below I queried him as to what was there, but he didn't respond. Anything that he found first would be his, and he needed time to decide. The roof pitch only allowed him to assume a crouched stance, and from this angle he could see that he had grossly underestimated the amount of stuff that was there. There were piles of old clothes, a Bible, some faded Readers Digest books, a set of blue and white dishes, a chipped porcelain skillet, an ironing board, a box of Christmas decorations, various sizes of mason canning jars, a vase of plastic flowers, a bedpan, a hula hoop, a radio with the knobs missing, a washtub, and much more of the same.

The overwhelming amount of rubble required him to kick debris as he walked, just to uncover floor space. A kick with his right foot moved a bag of something that caused a cloud of dust to stir. Before the dust could settle, his next kick made contact with another object. This time the object was solid and it moved only slightly. Looking down at his left foot, a tiny ray of light guided his eyes to what appeared to be a body part. A frantic rumble followed a frightening scream. Henry dove head first toward the attic opening. Never minding the stairs, he fell below to the cold vinyl-covered floor faster than he had ascended it. The impact of the fall should have meant a broken bone or two. At the very least it should have knocked the breath out of him, but it didn't. With his heart pounding profusely, he rolled onto his back and stammered, "There-there-there-there is-is some-some-body's leg-leg up-up there!" I said, "What?" Slowly and with more clarity he shouted, "There is a leg up there!" We quickly closed the attic door and waited until Mama got home. After investigating the incident, it was discovered that the previous owner, who was now deceased, was also an amputee. The prosthesis had been left behind when they moved. Henry's fright was so great that it cured his speech impediment and he never stuttered again.

After I left Union College I spent the next two years completing my degree at Clark College, yet another attempt to bide time while I decided what I wanted to do. This was also another opportunity for me to graduate and march down the aisle with a cap and gown. Fate didn't see it that way.

❧ TWO DARK CLOUDS ❧

I never had much of a relationship with my brother Calvin. He, like my older brothers eager to pursue a better life away from the house on Arcadia Circle, had joined the military at an early age. His military career was cut short when he was diagnosed with leukemia. At the age of twenty-eight, Calvin died on November 22, 1971. Henry had already begun his career of playing cat-and-mouse with the Georgia Correctional System, but they did give him a prison pass to attend the funeral. When my sister in New York died from an intestinal blockage exactly six weeks later, Henry was already at another facility, and that request to attend was denied.

———————

At the end of the winter semester of my senior year, I went to the registrar's office to verify that I was on target to complete all requirements necessary to graduate in the spring. To my surprise, no one could find my transcript. No one had any idea that I was even a registered student. I returned the following day to speak with Mrs. Eckta, the registrar. Mrs. Eckta was a short, heavyset woman who was well respected and equally feared. She prided herself in running a tight ship and was openly embarrassed about the flagrant discrepancy. Abruptly she dismissed me from her office and said, "I'll take care of it."

Several weeks passed without word from Mrs. Eckta. When I stopped by her office she was either not available or not in. It was obvious that I was being ignored. The second semester had already begun, the add/drop deadline was fast approaching, and I still had not heard from Mrs. Eckta. Once again I knew I needed to take the matter into my own hands, so I decided to schedule an appointment to speak with the college president, Dr. Vivian Henderson. This event was déjà vu. I had been in this space before, but so much about me had changed. Past disappointments had given me backbone. Better eyesight had given me a clearer insight. My stubbornness had given birth to a deeper resolve, and the sit-in movement of the '60s had given me a platform. On the next morning when I stepped inside of the administration building I stepped outside of myself. I was not even aware that I was no longer timid. Instead I was intrepid.

The entire right wing on the main floor housed the offices of the executive staff, the treasurer, and the registrar. The office door of the registrar was the only door open. Inside the outer office a receptionist greeted me and asked the nature of my visit. She immediately suggested that I speak with the registrar instead of Dr. Henderson. When I informed her that I had tried that route and now wanted to plead my case to a higher authority, she immediately went to Mrs. Eckta's office anyway, to see if there was an update. Mrs. Eckta's abrasive personality intimidated everyone. Absolutely no one, including her boss, questioned her decisions or directives. When Mrs. Eckta learned of my attempt to overshoot her authority, she was incensed. The receptionist returned with the response that Mrs. Eckta was busy and would call me when and if she had something to report. Two years ago I would have left with teary eyes and a bruised self-esteem, but it was time for someone else to share this pain. On that day I refused to be pushed aside.

With a crazed look in my eyes I pounded my fist on the wooden desk and adamantly shouted, "No! I am not moving. Someone will listen to me today!" At precisely the same moment, Dr. Henderson appeared in his doorway. His sudden appearance was either coincidental or a response to my loud ranting—which one, I will never know. From the corner of my eye, I saw Mrs. Eckta spring to her feet, but the president invited me into his office before she could move. Once seated inside the president's office, I became overwhelmed with nervousness.

I couldn't believe what I had just done. I had never talked that strongly to an adult before.

I was twenty-one years old and didn't know whether I would be expelled or jailed. My voice quivered as I explained my dilemma. While I was still babbling away, he picked up his phone and directed Mrs. Eckta to pull my transcript. Dr. Henderson's demeanor was quite a contrast to Mrs. Eckta's. His personality was not only inviting, it was engaging. The room was quiet. To fill the void and perhaps to calm me he asked, "What are your plans after graduation?"

To be truthful I had none. I knew that my first order of business was to move away from our house as soon as possible, but I couldn't tell him that. I knew what my friends had plans to do, so I felt safe repeating the same dialogue. I responded, "When I graduate I plan to get married, work two years, and then have two children." His comments to my reply startled me. He said, "Getting married and having children is serious business. Why do you feel you have to take those steps so soon?" I had no answer because I had no clue. He said, "If you don't want to or if you are not ready for marriage or children, don't feel pressured to do either."

By now my head was reeling. How did we get to this conversation? I didn't know answers to those questions. I couldn't even make an intelligent comment. I had actually been much like a parrot, mimicking what I had heard others say. And I had never heard anyone say what he was telling me. This conversation was clearly over my head. I think my mouth was open, but I'm sure nothing was coming out. He obviously saw how dumbstruck I was, so he rescued me by saying, "All I'm trying to say is, everyone is born an original but most people spend their entire life trying to be someone else's carbon copy. Don't feel that your life has to fit into boxes that someone else has built. Build your own."

Knuckles rapped lightly against his office door, and then Mrs. Eckta entered. She joined Dr. Henderson on the other side of his desk as they spoke in hushed tones about my transcript. What they were saying was no longer important because now I was in deep thought about the carbon paper and the original. Every woman was expected to get married and have babies. I never thought we had an option.

Mrs. Eckta turned to leave as Dr. Henderson turned to me. In resignation he said, "Miss Hill, I apologize for the confusion. Apparently one of your courses did not transfer from your former school. You still need another three credit hours to qualify for graduation." I was already carrying the maximum allowable credits, so adding another class was clearly out of the question. Therefore, marching in the upcoming graduation was out of the equation. Just like before I could not participate in my commencement. Unlike before, my life would be forever changed, because I had just been given permission and encouragement to color outside of the lines.

I already had a job offer so I completed the class off-site. My degree was conferred six months later.

———————

My journey to Nebraska for college had ignited my wanderlust, and I was anxious to move to Florida to take my first job. I was twenty-two years old and enjoying my first apartment in Orlando. I owned a car, and I had a managerial position with a major retailer. I still inwardly envied those girls in high school who already had boyfriends and by now were probably married with children.

Several years after I moved away I returned for a weekend visit to find that Atlanta was slowly becoming a growing metropolis. People were moving in from the North, and some were coming from smaller surrounding towns like Ludowici and Jakin, Georgia. I never saw anyone from my old neighborhood—no one from E. C. Clement Elementary and absolutely no one from Booker T's graduating class of '68. Everyone was a stranger.

A window booth at a downtown eatery gave me a panoramic view of the kaleidoscope of characters who walked the downtown streets of Atlanta. Within minutes my eyes became transfixed on a little girl waiting at a bus stop. She was the first person whom I recognized. Her skin was very fair; her sandy brown hair was long and coarse but neatly combed into three plaits. Her eyes were bright, and her ribbons and anklets matched her pinafore dress. She appeared to be seven or eight years old, but all of her features mirrored the image of someone my age, someone who had been a source of agitation in my life. Her hand was being held tightly by a woman who was not as recognizable, perhaps her mother. Like the little girl, the woman had fair skin. Her coarse hair was unkempt and pulled back from her face by a utility rubber band. Her clothes appeared to be almost two sizes too small, and each seam grinned to hold back her bulging girth. Her eyes were not bright; instead they were blurred. The woman was Gail, a former classmate.

Gail was one of the childhood ringleaders who taunted me at lunchtime with their ham sandwiches. It looked as if she'd had too many of them now. Her fair skin looked sallow and she looked old, inside and out. As adorable as Gail's little girl appeared to be, I no longer envied Gail for having so many boyfriends. Perhaps too many boyfriends and babies at an early age wasn't all it was cracked up to be. I recalled how I had bought her friendship by sharing my homework assignments. Even that was okay because I benefited in ways I could never have imagined.

On a more recent visit back home, navigating the five lanes of bustling traffic on Interstate 85 South, near the downtown Williams Street exit, was difficult because there was so much to see. I couldn't keep my eyes off the slick MARTA rail system flying through the air on my right and the massive electronic billboard on my left—a billboard that flashed the advantages of a Verizon cell phone and then a Chick-fil-A billboard with three black-spotted cows encouraging everyone to "Eat Mor Chikin" (as if Atlanta needed any encouragement).

The next sign alerted that Interstate 20 was approaching. Interstate 20 West is still the artery that channels folks to MLK Drive, which used to be Hunter Street, then on to Burbank Drive, then to Arcadia Circle, the street where I grew up. Staring out at the bustling city of Atlanta I watched people moving to and fro. I wondered if any of them had ever lived in the house at 97 Arcadia Circle and what stories they have to share about the second room on the right.

Memories of growing up there are becoming distant, but they are still deep. As memories flooded my mind, melancholy filled my space and a tear filled the corner of my eye. Once again, my tear ducts triggered my bladder, and I got off at the next exit to find the nearest restroom.

Epilogue

In my freshman English composition class at Union College we were given the writing assignment of drafting an essay about our first year in college. I don't remember what I wrote, but I do remember using a lot of metaphors describing the weather, the lay of the land, and the diverse cultures on the campus. I got an A on my paper. As a matter of fact, I got an A+. That was the only A that I ever got at the school. Perhaps that white instructor saw something in me that I did not see in myself until decades later.

To this very day I hate that I didn't get the name and address of that nice gentleman who came to my rescue in the O'Hare Airport. He would definitely be a permanent part of my Christmas card list. He may have told his family of the incident. If so, I hope one of them is reading this.

❦ FORGIVING DADDY ❦

In the preface of this manuscript I mentioned that although our book club was formed for the purpose of improving race relations among women, it did much more for me. For nine months each year, women of different races meet every fourth Sunday in each other's homes to have a lively discussion on a selected reading. We always try to select books that invite us to probe the similarities and differences in how we relate to other women and men in our lives. At one of our monthly meetings I finally released the long-held hatred that I carried for Daddy. It was also the weekend following the acquittal of O. J. Simpson. At the end of each book club session, Cathie Holcombe, our discussion leader, posed a thought for us to ponder in the days ahead. Her question at this particular meeting was, "What was one habit or mind-set that your parents tried to rid you of and one which you are glad they were unsuccessful in removing?" One by one each member shared her story. I began to search for cobwebs that I had been unable to clear. Instantly I thought of Daddy. I was quite proud of how I had grown over the last thirty years. I had truly released any hate that I harbored for former employers, coworkers, classmates, friends, and even former lovers. I actively encouraged others to do the same. I only thought of Daddy when others spoke lovingly of their own father. But the name "Daddy" still came out like the taste of a bad persimmon.

Perhaps Daddy was trying to rid me of my stubbornness, a character flaw that could prove deadly for blacks in the 1960s. History tells us how slave owners heaped cruel and unusual punishment on errant slaves. The quickest way to subdue a slave was to break his spirit. Castration, dismemberment, and mutilation worked better than death. Some think that Daddy may have been releasing pent-up frustrations from his job and pressures from an oppressive culture. Now that I think of it, I can never recall Daddy ever raising his voice or his hand to Mama. Perhaps he thought if he didn't, neither would any child that they raised. Others thought his behavior was a carryover from how he was disciplined as a child. It was probably a combination of all of these. It's doubtful that I'll ever know for sure. I was too stubborn to allow Daddy's razor strap to break my spirit. For that I am thankful. On that day of reckoning I felt stupid for allowing my life to be held prisoner by a now faceless person, a lifeless person who has long since turned to dust, one who is no longer a person but now just a concept in time. At that very moment I let it all go. The healing was complete.

History also tells us that Emory University Hospital in Atlanta performed its first heart surgery in the early 1960s. Perhaps Daddy's unsuccessful heart surgery two years later helped them to get it right. That, too, I will never know.

❦ HENRY ❦

Offense: Theft by receiving of stolen prop
Conviction County: Fulton County

Letters from Henry were always amusing because they came with a different alias and they were always a request for cash. Mama spent the last years of her life talking, begging, midnight praying, counseling, crying, weekend visiting, and spending hard-earned money trying to rescue her son Henry—a son who was well on his way to convincing himself that we were the ones who needed to be rescued. In the coming years the Georgia Correctional System tried unsuccessfully to make a model citizen out of Henry. Instead Henry was more successful in making a mockery out of the Georgia Correctional System.

A letter from Henry in 2007:

> Dear Linda,
> Well I guess you are saying, "What a surprise!" Yeah it's me, back in the Clayton County Correctional Center. My job at Kroger's didn't pan out. It only lasted for three weeks. It was too much confusion over me having two different names. I have to work in my real name. But I'm registered here as Henry Jackson. I'm hoping that when I get out again, you can introduce me to some of your friends. I'd like to hook up with a few rich or well-off older females who might be in need of a healthy young buck like me. While race is not important, my taste is slim, older females who are not as dark as me. If you see me with my arms around a fat woman, it's not what you think. I'm just holding her for the police. Can you send me one hundred dollars? My release month is April 2007. I promise to do right this time.
> Love your brother,
> Henry

One of the stories that he shared years later was about his involvement in a major auto theft ring. White men, who owned large car dealerships, secretly contracted him to steal new cars for resale. Henry said he could steal a car from a transport truck before the nipples wore off the tires. For a paltry fee, the white man paid other agents to alter the VIN numbers and change the locks. Since the car was not a part of the regular inventory, the dealership never paid taxes. The dealership offered the consumer a tremendous discount and subsequently sold more cars. The dealer, in turn, got a tremendous profit. Each thief in the crime ring specialized in stealing certain makes and models. Henry's specialty was Chevrolets. For each stolen car, Henry got one hundred dollars. That was good money for a young, uneducated black man in the '70s. When we expressed how unbelievable his story was, he said something that I'll never forget. He replied, "Surely you don't think that corruption starts at the bottom? The bottom is only where the punishment starts." When Henry was arrested for his high-speed chase through downtown Atlanta, he was out of jail within weeks. He knew the system. Maybe Henry was right when he said corruption starts at the top.

Over the years, all of my family described his escapades as scary, stupid, sorrowful, clever, dangerous, and some just downright funny. None of it was ever funny to Mama, for she had seen far too many instances where white police officers took every opportunity to wipe out a black life for even the smallest offense. She had already buried a husband. She could not stand the thought of burying a young son.

Over the last forty years all of my family members, including cousins, in-laws, and family friends, have tried to intervene to close the revolving prison door of release and return. On Henry's last release we held our breath, hoping, wishing, and praying that he was ready to turn over a new leaf. My sister put her life on hold to find him a job and get him enrolled in school. She got him a cell phone, transportation, work clothes, a bank account, and free room and board. For the first time in his life he became a registered voter. But trying to live on this side of the prison walls was tough. At the age of fifty-eight Henry was like a fish trying to swim out of water.

The computer had changed the entire world. A mouse was no longer just a pesky rodent. Every job required a background and drug screening. No one had or heard of a rotary telephone. There were now more than 100 TV channels. The vinyl long-playing and 45 rpm records had been replaced by a thin piece of plastic called CDs. Reel-to-reel films had been through many generations of media and replaced by DVDs, and email had replaced U.S. mail. Gasoline was no longer seventy-five cents per gallon. Every automobile had to be registered and have liability coverage. What was probably more devastating to Henry, more than anything else, was how his lack of computer knowledge prevented him from disassembling and rebuilding cars. Now when he steals a car, he just rides around until it gives out of gas. As of this writing, Henry is back in jail and, as always, under an assumed name. Public records indicate his offense is possession of tools to commit a crime.

Any projected release date is no more than a visitor's pass. Henry's eyes now look like my grandfather's eyes—flat, like fish eyes, with no life behind them. We no longer visit him; instead he visits us whenever time permits.

❦ THE ATTIC DOOR ❧

The second room on the right was the only room in the Arcadia Circle house that had four doors. In addition to the hall entry and the two adjoining wall doors, there was a fourth door that led to the attic. It was scary and creepy. I only remember opening the door once. A long flight of wooden steps rose to an open landing that was musty and damp. The stairs seemed steeper because there was no railing to hold on to. Walls of spider webs parted the space. Other walls were made visible only by a stream of light from a broken vent. Perhaps that broken vent was the portal for the resident bats and rodents. In the winter, you could hear the wind howl through the rafters. In the summer, the rats had a rodeo of their own. At least that is what I thought. No matter how much you know, there will always be the unknown. No matter what you say, you can never say it all. No matter what you do, you can never do it all. When someone takes a misstep in life, no one knows whether or when that person will get back on the right track.

❧ SIBLING UPDATE ❧

Over the years, each of my siblings led interesting lives, and each could probably tell more fascinating stories. Friends and neighbors have described all of
us as bright and naturally talented. Mama believed that education was the key
that unlocked our potential, so she promised to support our efforts to attend
college if we wanted to go. Eight of her eleven children took the plunge. Melvin
Jr. was one of the few men of that time to be admitted to Morehouse College
at the age of sixteen. Janie earned a track scholarship to Tuskegee Institute, and
she competed in several track meets with Olympian Wilma Rudolph. Charles
earned a tennis scholarship to Tuskegee—also something unheard of for poor
blacks in the early '60s. Some say he was as good as tennis great Arthur Ashe.
It's ironic that the same disease claimed both of their lives. Lettie attended
Oakwood College and Sarah went to Morris Brown College. Much later, at
the age of sixty, Sarah returned to school to study plumbing. She became the
oldest woman to ever finish the program at the Mechanical Trades Institute in
Atlanta. She was also the first civilian woman with a skilled trade ever to volunteer to work in Iraq under Haliburton, the government contractor. Calvin
and I studied at Clark College. Gary, the youngest, attended the University
of Georgia. History records that he became the first black male to earn an
undergraduate degree in landscape architecture from that school. At the age of
sixty-one, I became the first published author in my family.

❧ MAMA ❧

Forty-five years after Mama left school, when her youngest child had graduated
from high school, she returned to complete her studies. Since Mama worked
at night she wanted to go to school in the daytime but that required breaking some rules. At the time, day school was only for students eighteen years
and younger. Night school was designated for anyone older and those who
had taken up adult ways, such as having a baby out of wedlock or working to

Mama receives her high school diploma at age sixty-five, May 25, 1977

support a family. Mama must have quietly observed the many strategies I used with the school's administration to get them to veer from tradition because she used the same tactics to plead her case. But just like me, she was unable to convince the rigid school board. Undaunted she began her four-year journey to night school to fulfill a lifelong dream of earning her high school diploma.

At the age of sixty-five, Mama received her high school diploma from Booker T. Washington High Night School. She was also noted for having perfect attendance and being on the yearbook staff. On that special night in May 1977 Mama delivered the graduation speech and recited Kipling's poem "If." To my knowledge, that was the only poem that Mama ever fully committed to memory.

Mama was a teacher—not the formal one of her dreams but one she could not have imagined. Mama was a professor in the school of hard knocks: leading by example, molding our minds, minding our manners, disciplining our diversions, acknowledging a Higher Power, and never grading on the curve.

The head injuries that Mama sustained in the 1970 car accident may have triggered the onset of Alzheimer's disease. We may never know for sure. When Mama was brought to Greensboro in 1986 she had already begun her struggle with dementia. I agreed to assume her custodial care.

I could feel the stiffness gradually ease from my neck as I turned onto the two-lane drive that led away from the bustling five lanes of traffic on Wendover Avenue. Wendover Avenue provides access to the eastern and western quadrants of Greensboro, and every building could be seen from the street—well, almost every building. The Evergreens Senior Healthcare facility was the exception. There was no billboard, no flashing lights, and no fancy jingle, only a simple white sign with green lettering, one pine tree, and street numbers.

As my car approached the end of the driveway, I entered a vacuum that sucked out the smell of gasoline, the toxic fumes of exhaust pipes, and the tensions of every anxious motorist. The mature trees and hardy foliage cleansed the air that now felt serene and fresh.

It was late August 1987, and the six-acre campus of the Evergreens was pretty and inviting. The grounds were manicured, and the hardy hosta and monkey grass played leapfrog along the walkway. A hummingbird feeder buzzed with activity, and a squirrel rolled acorns across a park bench. This place was Mama's new home, her last one—such a stark contrast to the one on Arcadia Circle, and a cruel irony that the only way she came to live here in a place so peaceful was only because her mind had already gone someplace else. Less than eight years after Mama left Atlanta, I learned that the world was coming to Atlanta again, this time in Mama's own backyard.

Two decades after King's death, the face of Atlanta remained largely unchanged for the good. The rich got richer, the poor got poorer, and those in between struggled harder to put up a good front.

Parts of the city were so dark at night that locals felt threatened and tourists stayed away. In almost every part of the city, traffic lights were out of sync; bridges and roads were in desperate need of repair. This status-seeking city had little else to boast except Underground Atlanta and the Martin Luther King Jr. Memorial. Large groups of tourists came to visit the King National Historic

Site but not many came to make Atlanta their home. The thrill of Underground Atlanta was alluring, but the conditions above ground were still appalling.

The tarpaper shack in Vine City that once belonged to Grandpa Hill was still standing. Most of the original neighbors on Arcadia Circle were dead and gone. Building codes had changed but were not enforced. Rainwater still stood ankle-deep after a hard storm.

When Mama's siblings could no longer keep her family's homestead, she moved back to Summerhill, one of the worst ghettos in Atlanta. Long after black politicians were sworn into office, Summerhill (located within walking distance of downtown) was still a bevy of abandoned lots, decrepit houses, and cracked sidewalks. Eight years after Mama began her struggle with Alzheimer's, the house that she struggled so hard to keep in her family was vacant, condemned, and used regularly by drug pushers and prostitutes. That was about to change.

In September 1991, Atlanta learned that it had won the right to host the 1996 Summer Olympic Games. I couldn't believe it. The Olympics would actually be held in my hometown!

Newspapers were full of stories about how Atlanta would no longer be referred to as a "town" but would become a "city." Determined to become known as the icon of the New South in just five short years, Atlanta launched an all-out effort to improve its blighted neighborhoods and reverse one hundred years of urban decay. Big businesses all pitched in to give the city a facelift.

The enthusiasm grew, and the city seemed to take on a magic synergy. Although deeply rooted in Greensboro, hundreds of miles away, I could feel the groundswell of excitement all the way up there. Olympics mania was spreading fast, and the Coca-Cola Bottling Company wanted to help spread it faster. To add fuel to this fire, Coca-Cola sponsored a contest: "Coca-Cola Wants to Give Your Face Its Place in Atlanta."

In celebration of the 1996 Centennial Olympic Games, a mural would be painted on the wall of a fifteen-story building in the historic Summerhill neighborhood. The mural would contain approximately forty faces of

Atlanta-area residents, selected to reflect the multicultural diversity of Atlanta and the spirit of the Olympic Games.

In 1994, they began looking for neighbors from all across the world who called Atlanta home. The contest rules were simple: "Send in your story or that of a friend in 200 words or less. Tell why they call Atlanta home and what the results of living there had meant to them." My sister Sarah decided to enter a poem about Mama.

ODE TO MISS MARY
(edited version)

She was second eldest of fourteen,
Tho' a high school dropout at sixteen;
Never forgot her childhood dream,
To become a teacher of high esteem.
Widowed by a surgeon's hand,
Duty-bound to raise her dependent clan;
All of whom she bore and weaned,
Taught each to be respectful and clean
When her youngest was grown and educated
She was tired but even more persuaded;
To fulfill her childhood dream,
to become a teacher of high-esteem
After fifty years of ambition on hold,
She returned to class to capture the gold.
Grasping anything her instructors could teach,
On graduation night she delivered the commencement speech.
At the age of 65,
she received her diploma,
the long awaited prize.
Her contributions to Atlanta were many,
And never asked a charity's penny;
Always first to say, "I will,"
Such a person was Mary Lee Hill

Mama's poem was chosen as a finalist, and a personal interview would determine the winner. Mama was now settled in Greensboro, and her condition had begun to decline. She was too fragile to travel back to Atlanta to interview, and she was eliminated from the competition. Several years later, a friend told me that the image of one of the winners bore a strong resemblance to Mama. Summerhill, which once symbolized the utter despair of black people in the South, now has been registered and given historical

A weekend visit at The Evergreens

status. Unfortunately the pages of history will be void of the stories of many strong black women like Mama who helped stitch the multicultural quilt that was the covering for so many who would one day make Atlanta great.

During my weekend visits at the Evergreens, I spent many hours revisiting the past and trying desperately to keep Mama in the present.

For fifteen years, small family gatherings with cake and cards was how we celebrated each birthday. When her feeble condition prevented that from happening, I still searched for other ways to acknowledge the milestones. Just before her verbal communication ended, she said the funniest and most telling things.

By her eighty-sixth birthday, she spent her days staring at the floor, looking at nothing. It was obvious that life had long left her and words no longer had meaning, or so I thought. But I was stubborn. I prodded her, "What do you want for your birthday, Mama?" I got no response. The next time I suggested, "Do you want some cake?" She was still detached and lifeless. Knowing how much she loved ice cream, I prompted once again, "Can I get you some ice cream?" Mama still did not flinch. In a last-ditch playful attempt to elicit any kind of response, I asked, "Can I get you a boyfriend?" That question was the lightning rod that brought her head to an upright position, and her voice became as clear as a bell when she responded, "Oh no. I ain't got nothing for no man to do." Perhaps there were still some cobwebs that Mama had been unable to clear also. When I recovered from my sidesplitting laughter, Mama had already returned to her world of silence.

It was the first week in November 2000, and all of Greensboro was enjoying an Indian summer. The last few months of blistering temperatures were difficult for everyone, but the last winter of Mama's life was difficult for her and me. The euphoric seventy-eight-degree day this close to winter was an unexpected treat. It gave me time to get my mind ready for the transition.

The weather is only one of the many good reasons to live in the Piedmont. The major arteries that lead to the heart of the city are cleverly disguised as interstates and highways. Along the stretch of highway to Chapel Hill, a wonderful sense of extravagance abounds in the mass planting of beautiful, hardy wildflowers. The vibrant colors of white poppies, gold and orange marigolds, and red and purple lilies are breathtaking. A stone's throw from Winston-Salem, the soft shoulders of the embankments are brushed with a nostalgic mix of golden marguerites; fuchsia flow beneath rows and rows of variegated crepe myrtles. On the North Carolina road to Julian and Liberty, golden forsythia shrubs announce the first sign of spring and cast a bright light on the honeysuckle and wild blackberries growing at their feet. Even the bales of hay and tobacco fields add charm to the short drive to Browns Summit.

❦ GREENSBORO ❧

The name fits. Everything in this borough is green and growing. Living in Greensboro was good, and since moving here from Atlanta I found it easy to claim this city as home.

The night before my house was jumping with laughter and good times.

Every room overflowed with friends and food. That's how black folks celebrate. Like the ending of the seasons, Mama's season of life had come to an end. My friends came to celebrate Mama's life when they heard she had died.

Earlier that year in February, when her doctor summoned me to her bedside, he said her condition was so fragile there was no way that she could survive more than a week. Well, he didn't know Mama. She rallied for eight months longer before she left us on October 31. On the night of her passing, her physician said that her heartbeat was still the strongest of anyone else in the entire 300-bed facility. That same determined heartbeat still beats strongly within me. Room 318 was the only room that she occupied for her last fifteen years, the same number of years that I occupied the second room on the right.

Several days later and 750 miles away in Chicago, Illinois, Aunt Nell, her last surviving sibling, lay gravely ill in Mercy Hospital. Because of Aunt Nell's fragile condition, we purposely decided not to tell her of Mama's passing. Later we learned from her attending physician that on that very day Aunt Nell sat straight up in her hospital bed and said, "I've got to go somewhere." The doctor asked, "Where do you have to go, Mrs. Johnson?" To that she replied, "I've got to meet somebody." With those last words, Aunt Nell leaned back in her bed, closed her eyes, and joined Mama.

It was four decades before Lettie and I spoke of the bedroom incident again. She said the only thing she remembers is that her panties were always down when she woke up. She also said that Mama's reaction to that incident created a silent wedge between her and Mama. That wedge remained for the remainder of their lives. I never got a chance to tell Mama what I saw. She wasn't ready to receive it then. She probably never would have been ready. Fifty years later I asked my older brother if he remembered the incident. Without hesitation he responded, "Yes, I do." Then finally I heard him say what I thought I heard him think back in 1964. He said, "That was not a healthy sleeping arrangement."

When Reverend George W. Brooks eulogized Mama, he likened her to a sweet Georgia peach. He said, "A peach comes from a seed and a peach seed is not something people save and relish. As a matter of fact a peach seed is something rough, not glamorous or cute. The life of Mary Hill could be likened to that of a peach seed. Isn't it amazing how God hides good stuff in things that don't look good to others? But only God knows what the end product is going to be."

More than a decade after her passing my friends remember her as Miss Mary; family members remember her as Mary. She is still present at all family gatherings as we fondly recall and repeat all of her funny and wisdom-filled sayings. To all of her children she will always be remembered as Mama.

❧ BOOKER T. WASHINGTON HIGH ❦

This statute is located in front of Booker T. Washington High School in Atlanta, Georgia. It was placed there in 1927. It is the exact replica of the Booker T. Washington Memorial on the campus of Tuskegee University in Tuskegee, Alabama.

The mighty Bulldogs of Washington High are still "lifting the veil of ignorance."

JEFFREY M. FRANK / SHUTTERSTOCK.COM

The school still stands, but today it is much different. A metal detection system and armed officers guard its entrance. Inside its corridors everything seems so small. The location and layout of the main office are still the same. The same room-length wooden counter partitions the open space. On one side of it a young and professional administrative staff openly welcomes each student. Each name is always prefaced with Mr. or Miss.

Sultry songstress Lena Horne and comedian Nipsy Russell attended this school. To chronicle the school's illustrious history, a special room displaying artifacts from

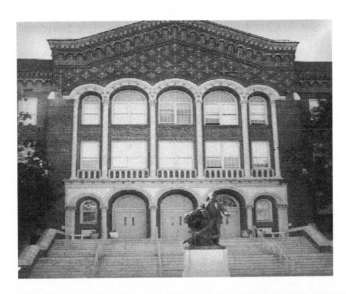

The graduating class of 1968
The vacant seat on the top row, over the number eight, was mine.

1924 to the present has been created. My homeroom was once located in that same room. Framed photos of past commencement exercises are displayed in chronological order.

It's interesting to note that the framed photo of the graduating class of 1968 (my class) is missing. No one knows why. Decades later I learned that my classmates did not know I was missing from the graduation either.

I didn't see any portraits of students who graduated from night school. They were also an invisible part of the school's history. Maybe they were there somewhere, but they certainly didn't get the spotlight attention. History also records that my first cousin, Dr. Robert L. Collins, served as the school's fifth principal. As of this writing, my niece, Dr. Vanessa Nason, sits at the helm as the school's tenth principal.

❦ 97 ARCADIA CIRCLE ❦

The shotgun house played a role in the folklore and culture of the South. Folklore has it that spirits are attracted to shotgun houses because they may pass straight through them and that some houses are built with doors intentionally misaligned to deter these spirits.

The house at 97 Arcadia Circle still stands. Nothing much has changed except the exterior paint color. Grass now grows in the front yard spot where I once played. A home security sign is posted in the yard. I wonder if that sign is meant for humans on the outside or for spirits on the inside.

Decades later, we still talk about living there. When we do, we all refer to it only as "97."

Many years later I realized why our house seemed so close to the neighboring house. Both houses sat close to the adjoining property line. My bedroom, the second room on the right, aligned with the neighbor's kitchen.

After I moved to North Carolina, local optometrists could no longer grind lenses thick enough to correct my sight. It was at the Duke University Eye Center in Durham, North Carolina,

From left to right: Mama, Myrna in front, me (with my new glasses), and Gary, with the round head (I don't remember this picture being taken, but it was more than forty years after I left Atlanta before I saw it.)

that I learned that I have an extreme form of nearsightedness called kerataconus. It was also at Duke Eye Clinic that I learned that, without corrective lenses, I am legally blind.

You may find this hard to believe, but every time I go back to Atlanta and see the Coca-Cola Bottling sign near Georgia Tech and the Grant Park Zoo sign near Turner Field, the first and only thing that comes to mind are the field trips that I missed. To this very day, I have never been to a symphony. Now that I can well afford to attend, I no longer care to.

I don't know exactly when I became comfortable in my own skin. I am certain that the James Brown era of "Say it loud, I'm black and I'm proud," and the Afro and braids regime contributed to my metamorphosis. But the true change had to come from within. That internal change didn't happen overnight or as a result of any one traumatic experience. Instead it came in snatches, often subtle, always unexpected.

Twenty-two years after leaving Atlanta, my decision to pursue a graduate degree was prompted partly by my desire to achieve more discipline and direction in my life. Honestly, I think I still had a deeper desire to march down someone's aisle wearing a cap and gown, but this time wasn't déjà vu. Instead it was déjà voodoo! I knew exactly how many credit hours were required. I knew exactly what courses had to be taken and when they were being taught. I reviewed the course catalog often and followed each directive diligently.

In the final semester when I attempted to register for the one remaining course that I needed to fulfill my requirements, I learned that the course would not be offered due to low enrollment. I could not believe it. I felt as if a dark cloud had been hovering over my head for almost a quarter of a century. I checked with every local school in the UNC system trying to get the class, but it was not available.

Commencement exercises at North Carolina A&T were similar to those at most universities: the event was primarily ceremonial. The official degree was conferred as a group at another designated time and place. My professor and my classmates knew of my dilemma but none of them knew of my past and pain. My professor assured me that I could take the class in the summer and my degree would be conferred in the winter. That was not good enough. I was tired of being deferred. I wanted to be conferred. I wanted the ceremony!

It was the Friday before Mother's Day. The campus was abuzz with spring and the anticipation of commencement. I still had not accepted my fate. I was still stupid with stubbornness. I was determined to be in that lineup on graduation morning, with or without a degree.

❧ THE DOORS ❧

The entry door swung inward on its hinges most nights and all days. As was the custom for shotgun houses, each room also had pass-through doors. These interior doors provided access to adjoining rooms without having to go back through an unheated hallway. Nothing ever passed through the pass-through doors in my room because they were blocked by beds. Each door had a keyhole, but no keys. None of them had locks. The pass-through doors had hinges and no locks, but they were always blocked. It's good if a door is not locked or blocked, but if it is, sometimes you have to kick the door open.

It was now less than twelve hours away from the commencement exercise and ten minutes before close-of-business for the bookstore. With only five minutes to spare I circumvented the system and finagled a cap and gown out of the bookstore staff.

On Saturday morning I was lightheaded with exhilaration as I finally stood beside my classmates waiting to march into the Greensboro Coliseum. I had never been this close before. I wanted to be seen but also took comfort that I would not be discerned amid the sea of caps and gowns. I thought, *Nothing can stop me now.* I turned around and stared straight into the eyes of my professor. There she stood in the next line, wearing a cap and gown. I didn't know that professors lined up and marched also. She was obviously just as surprised to see me. My heart quickened as I anticipated her command to leave the lineup. She asked, "How did you get in this line?" At that very instant the band loudly struck the opening chord of "Pomp

Cap and gown, at last, May 1994

and Circumstance" and I silently mouthed my reply, "I'll tell you later." I knew I never would. As the line inched into the auditorium, I held my head high and proudly marched down the aisle in my cap and gown. When I walked across the stage, the chancellor extended his hand with congratulations. I knew the gods were finally with me.

I once heard a minister say, "It is physically impossible to have a mountain without a valley." I interpreted that to mean that you cannot know the fullness of any emotion or any situation unless you can compare it to another extreme. There is no good without bad, no right without wrong, and no life without death. I began to view people and life's challenges differently. I have learned that heartache, disappointment, sadness, and even death are not something earmarked just for sinners or poor people. Tribulation is all a part of this thing called life. I have a choice whether I will allow hard times and setbacks to make me bitter or better. Each day I strive to choose the latter.

Daddy's death didn't just mean the end of horrific beatings. It also provided the means for me to get corrective eyewear that improved my sight. Another cruel irony of life: look how many had to die before America saw the light.

It was many years after leaving Atlanta before I understood Mama's saying about "an unwed pregnant girl and a broken leg." Those were the fast girls who pranced around like stallions but ended up breaking a leg. The huge responsibility of being a single parent was likened to the massive weight of a horse. A horse with a broken leg is unable to stand. An unwed teen in the 1960s faced similar odds. For both, life would never come easy.

Each time that I remember the book club discussion that challenged me to think of a habit or mind-set that my parents tried to rid me of, I remember the headstrong and stubborn little girl who grew up at 97 Arcadia Circle. Although I was physically undersized, visually challenged, and self-conscious, I was also autonomous. Nevertheless, there was much about that nearsighted, nappy-haired child that I admired: her ability to adapt, her resolve to be resilient, and her refusal to conform. Sometimes those qualities work to my detriment. All of the time, they get me through tough times.

Society values cooperation over independence, obedience over individuality, and niceness above all else. But nice women seldom make history. Therein lies the rub. Remembering the struggles encountered at 97 Arcadia Circle is no longer painful. In almost every aspect of life, anything that can hurt you also has the ability to help you if you let it. Sometimes it takes a lifetime to understand what helped and what hurt.

When my formative years are compared to those of my contemporaries and certainly to the youth of today, it may appear that much of my childhood was lost, growing up in the second room on the right. If Mama were alive today, I'm sure she would say, "Lin, if you can learn a lesson from a loss, then you haven't lost a thing." Another one of her sayings.

Aftermath

I'll never forget Dr. Henderson at Clark College. I Googled his name and found this:

A TRIBUTE TO DR. VIVIAN W. HENDERSON:

ECONOMIST AND EDUCATOR

By James A. Hefner

> Dr. Henderson's philosophy of higher possibilities was evident in his writings.... One finds in his writings that economics was important to him only as long as it related to furthering an understanding of the conditions under which his people were forced to live.... He had a deep and abiding concern for Blacks in general. (A tribute read at the American Economic Association meeting, Atlantic City, New Jersey, September 17, 1976)

Every opportunity I get, I build my own boxes and I color outside of the lines. Today, not only am I proud of my black skin, I purposely choose bold, brilliant colors to highlight its dark hue. Even though the present fashion trend is braids, weaves, extensions, and wigs, I proudly keep my hair cut short, sometimes close to a razor burn.

As I write this book, I think that being denied an opportunity to march in my high school graduation was part of the master plan, perhaps prophetic or at the very least predestined. Had I marched down that aisle in 1968 and experienced the artificial and temporary high of the ceremony I probably would have ended my educational pursuit and married my high school sweetheart. Had I marched at Clark College I may have never pursued a graduate degree.

In my relentless pursuit to march in a commencement exercise, I gained more than a graduate degree. It was at North Carolina A&T State University that I began to understand and embrace the social science of lifelong learning. All of the experiences that I perceived as setbacks, setups, and upsets in my family, the community, the schools, and religious institutions were instead teachable moments, cleverly disguised as treacherous mountains. The conflicts of my past were a platform for my future.

I no longer lament the struggles; instead I celebrate them. My stubbornness and determination are firmly rooted in the furrowed ground of a difficult childhood, failed relationships, missed opportunities, denied jobs, and disappointments.

More than half a century later, whenever I see a puppy chained or fenced in a yard, unable to roam freely, I feel his despair. Every time I see a battered or abused child, a lonely and confused child, a helpless child, any child whose fate lies totally at the mercy of an uncaring adult, I remember my days at Miss Dorothy's house.

Every time I pass a large car dealership, I wonder how many of those cars are stolen. When I became aware that auto VIN numbers are now virtually immovable, I wonder what prompted that move.

Whenever I see large numbers of black men caught in the revolving door of so-called reform, I wonder if their families were just as supportive, just as hurt and equally frustrated as our family was.

Whenever I encounter a pregnant teen, I wonder if Mama was right about the weight of her responsibility.

It was April 19, 1990, 7:18 a.m. A loud explosion was the last sound that I heard before time stopped. The piercing siren of an ambulance was the smelling salt that brought me back. As the paramedics gingerly positioned my limp body on a stretcher, a policeman stood nearby directing traffic and a news camera was already giving live coverage of the three-car accident at Holden Road and Interstate 85 South. As the ambulance sped toward Wesley Long Hospital, the EMT radioed ahead that a forty-year-old black female was conscious. Her vital signs were good, but there was head trauma. He added, "She says she's not pregnant but she is clutching her torso in pain."

Inside the emergency room, another team spun into action, shifted me onto a gurney, and raced to the trauma center. A bright round light swung overhead, my lifeless body lay below, and my ten acrylic fingernails lay broken to the quick. Slithers of broken glass that peppered my hair and face and my swollen cranium were external indications that my internal injuries could be worse. As the team prepared me for more X-rays, scissors clipped away at my clothing, and several pairs of hands tugged to remove my undergarments. Seconds before I lost consciousness, I craned my stiff neck toward the other end of the examination table to see if my underwear was clean!

To change my past would change me. At long last, I like me. I wouldn't take nothin' for my journey.

❧ THE CLOSETS ❧

There were no closets in the second room on the right or any room in that house. Our clothes hung from hooks and nails mounted behind the doors. Clothing that we used often was stored beneath our bed. Clothing and all other household items that were not in immediate use were piled high in the back hallway and hidden beneath a sheet, spread, or quilt.

Closets have skeletons. Skeletons are hidden stories.

Everyone has a story to tell.

I just told mine.

ACKNOWLEDGMENTS

Thanks to all my family, not only for your love and approval of the writing of this book, but also for making my life book-worthy.

Thanks to Cathie Holcombe, Maxine Baxter. Marie Castillo, Eileen Curry, Pearl Durham, Jean Bright, Barbara Hall, Gloria Harris, Gloria Bauman, Hattie Howell, Janet Inman, Anne Keith, Rhe Markham, Eugenia Perkins, Margaret Pipkin, Annie Purcell, Sally Morris-Randall, Mary Nell Smith, Tangela Stanley, Linda Whisnant, Kip Lester, and all the other ladies in the WIRR (Women Improving Race Relations) book club who encouraged me to start this journey and supported me along the way.

A special thanks to Dorothy Merchant for your eagle eye, sharp mind, compliments, and critique. Love you, girl!

Thanks to Kwami Osei Moyo (Thomas Saunders) who strongly encouraged me to pen my past and pushed me forward by saying, "Just get on with it."

Thanks to the publication *Now Write*, edited by Sherry Ellis. Your exercises and examples helped me immensely in fine-tuning this manuscript.

Thanks to everyone who has touched my life. Many of you have knowingly or unknowingly provided the script for this book.

DISCUSSION QUESTIONS

Linda Joyce channeled her life's negatives into writing about her world as a child.

1. What was creative or positive in Linda's world?

2. What was distorted in Linda's world?

3. What brought wholeness to Linda's world?

4. What boundaries did Linda encounter, real or imagined?

5. How did each of the following influence Linda at the time they occurred, and what brought about the eventual changes in her personality?
   - Bullying at school
   - Her first trip (to New York City)
   - World events (such as the assassination of JFK)
   - Personal loss (such as the death of her father)
   - Disappointments (such as being denied the opportunity to march at her graduations)

6. What events shaped your life?

7. How did the teachers in Linda's life—Mrs. Branch, Miss Carter, and Laura Woods—leave their marks on her life? What marks have teachers left on your own life?

8. Discuss Linda's visit with the Clark College president. What gifts did he give her? Has anyone ever given you similar gifts?

9. Mama disciplined with "sayings." Which sayings resonated with you and why?

10. Linda describes herself as a stubborn child. What are examples of this stubbornness? What other words would you use to describe Linda as a child, a teenager, a college student? Name some of the qualities you see, and back them up with examples from the book.

11. Mama plays an extremely important part in Linda's story. She is credited with being the stable force in Linda's life. How do you see Mary Lee Hill?

What was the best thing she gave Linda? How does she compare with your own mother or the person who raised you?

12. Linda states that she wanted to be like her mother in some ways and unlike her in other ways. What ways did you want to be like or unlike your mother or the person who raised you?

13. Linda uses vivid descriptions and comparisons in her story. What are some of your favorite expressions or descriptions of her world?

14. The author talks about becoming "comfortable in her own skin." What are the steps in her life that allowed this to happen? Are you comfortable in your own skin?

Made in the USA
Columbia, SC
20 May 2020